THE FEDERAL RESERVE CONSPIRACY

by Antony C. Sutton

First Printing: Copyright © 1995 Antony C. Sutton

All rights reserved. No part of this book may be reproduced in any form by any means without permission of the publisher, except brief quotes used in conjunction with reviews written especially for inclusion in a magazine, newspaper, or for educational purposes.

Reprint Edition: 2014 by Dauphin Publications Inc.
ISBN: 978-1-939438-09-6

Printed in the United States of America

Chapter One

THE BANKERS' BANK

Since 1913 politicians and media have treated the Federal Reserve Bank as a kind of untouchable off limits semi-God...no one except certified crackpots and kooks criticizes the Fed. Conventional wisdom dictates that *anyone* who attacks the Federal Reserve System is doomed and Congressional investigation of the Fed would result in economic chaos and a disastrous plunge in the stock market.

Recently President Clinton got to appoint Alan Blinder to a seat on the seven-member Board of Governors. Blinder launched into criticism of Fed actions, i.e., interest rates are too high and differed from the policy laid down by Chairman Alan Greenspan.

Poor Blinder was blindsided by the establishment press and no doubt received advice to keep quiet because since this initial speech, Blinder has repeatedly stated there are no differences between himself and Chairman Greenspan and *refuses to go* beyond this curious mea culpa.

There is a vast misconception about the Fed. The President and the Congress have very little, if any, influence on policy. The Congress handed over all monetary powers to the Fed in 1913. The Fed is *a private* bank, owned by banks, and pays dividends on its shares owned only by banks. The Fed is a private Bankers' Bank.

Yet Fed policy, not *Government* policy, is the dominant factor in economic growth. The Fed can create jobs by loosening credit. The Government talks a lot about creating jobs but in fact can only create bureaucracies which restrict rather than promote enterprise. The private sector creates productive jobs and the private sector is heavily dependent on Fed policy to do this.

The Congress has never investigated the Fed and is highly unlikely to do so. No one sees Fed accounts; they are not audited. No balance sheets are issued. No one, *but no one,* ever criticizes the Fed and survives.

Why all the secrecy and caution? Simply because the Fed has a *legal monopoly of money* granted by Congress in 1913 proceedings that were unconstitutional and fraudulent. Most of Congress had no idea of the contents of the Federal Reserve Bill signed by President Woodrow Wilson who was in debt to Wall Street.

The Federal Reserve has the power to create money. This money is fiction, created out of nothing. This can be money in the form of created credit through the discount window at which other banks borrow at the discount rate of interest or it can be notes printed by the Treasury and sold to the Fed and paid for by Fed-created funds

In brief, this private group of bankers has a money machine monopoly. This monopoly is uncontrolled by anyone and is guaranteed profit. Further, the monopoly doesn't have to answer questions or produce books or file annual statements.

It is an unrestricted money monopoly.

This book explains how this money monopoly came about. Obviously, Congress and the general public were misled and lied to when the Federal Reserve Bank was in discussion. Why the monopoly has continued is that the public is lazy, and so long as their individual world is reasonably fulfilling, has no reason to question Fed actions.

Even if they do they will find few books that surface the real facts. Academicians are too interested in protecting the Fed monopoly. An academic book criticizing the Fed will never find a publisher and the economist author would probably find tenure denied.

This is the first book that details hour by hour the events that led up to passage of the Federal Reserve Act of 1913 - and the many decades of work and secret planning that private bankers had invested to obtain their money monopoly.

The Federal Reserve Conspiracy

Los Angeles Times Cartoon by Ed Gamble, 1994

Chapter Two

THOMAS JEFFERSON AND THE MONEY POWER

It is fashionable in our contemporary academic world to ignore the powerful arguments of the Founding Fathers: the arguments of Presidents Thomas Jefferson, James Madison, and Andrew Jackson in particular. These arguments are that the Republic and the Constitution are always in danger from the so- called "money power," a group of autocrats, an elite we would call them today, who have manipulated the political power of the state to gain a monopoly over money issue.

Our modern academics even ignore Thomas Jefferson's chief reason for remaining in politics, i.e., to save the newly born United States from those elitists Jefferson called "monocrats" and "monopolists." It was the banking monopoly that Jefferson considered to be the greatest danger to the survival of the Republic.

The Jeffersonian ideal, one that contemporary elitists and Marxists sneer at, was a Republic comprising small property owning citizens (Marx would later call them bourgeoisie and Nelson Rockefeller used to call them "peasants") with a sense of civic awareness and a regard for the rights of their neighbors. The best government for Jefferson was the least government, where individual citizens take it upon themselves to protect the rights of neighbors. While Jefferson rejected socialist ideas he equally rejected the monopoly power of banking interests and feared what elitist banking power would do to American liberties. Said Jefferson:

> If the American people ever allow the banks to control the issuance of their currency, first by inflation and then by deflation, the banks and corporations that will grow up around them will deprive the people of all property until their children will wake up homeless on the continent their fathers occupied. The issuing power of money should be taken from the banks and restored to Congress and the people to whom it belongs. I sincerely believe the banking institutions are more dangerous to liberty than standing armies.[1]

The First Private Banking Monopoly

The Founding Fathers' discussion of banks and the money power reflect the clash of political philosophies among early Americans with Alexander Hamilton on one side and Jefferson, Madison and Franklin on the Jeffersonian side. Hamilton represented the autocratic tradition prominent in Europe that figured on winning through a banking monopoly what could not be won politically. It was Hamilton who introduced a bill in December, 1790 into the House of Representatives to grant a charter for the privately owned Bank of the United States, thus creating the first private money monopoly in the U.S., a predecessor to the privately owned Federal Reserve System. And it was Alexander Hamilton who just a few years before wrote the charter for the Bank of New York, the first bank in New York City. Isaac Roosevelt, great-great-grandfather Thomas Jefferson and the Money Power of Franklin Delano Roosevelt, was its second president, from 1796- 1791.

The Hamiltonian proposal for a national bank was a charter for private monopoly, a Congressional grant for a privileged few. The Bank of the U.S. had the sole right to issue currency, it was exempt from taxation, and the U.S. government was ultimately responsible for its actions and debts. As described by George Bancroft:

> *Hamilton recommended a National Bank with a capital of ten or fifteen million dollars, to be paid one-third in hard money and the other two-thirds in European funds or landed security. It was to be erected into a legal corporation for thirty years, during which no other bank, public or private, was to be permitted. Its capital and deposits were to be exempt from taxation, and the United States, collectively and particularly, were to become conjointly responsible for all its transactions. Its sources of profit were to be the sole right of issuing a currency for the United States equal in amount to the whole capital stock of the bank.* (2)

Public reaction to Congressional grant of a private banking monopoly for a group of private citizens was caustic. Declared James Madison:

> *In case of a universal circulation of the notes of the proposed bank, the profits will be so great that the government ought to receive a very considerable sum for granting the charter.*
>
> *There are other defects...and the right to establish subordinate banks ought not to be delegated to any set of men*

under Heaven. (3)

In the Senate, William McClay made a strong denunciation:

Jan. 17 (1790) Monday. I told them plainly that I was no advocate of the banking system; that I considered them machines for promoting the profits of unproductive Men;...that the whole profit of the bank ought to belong to the public, provided it was possible to advance the whole stock on her account.

But I must remark that the public was grossly imposed upon in the present instances. While she (Ed: the public,) *advanced all specie; individuals* (Ed: the bank organizers) *advanced three-fourths in certificates, which were of no more value in the support of the bank than so much stubble. Besides, the certificates were all under interest already, and it was highly unjust that other paper (money) should be issued on their credit which bore a premium and operated as a further tax on the country.* (4)

Hamilton's proposal was referred to a Senate Committee. But this Committee included Philip Schyler (Hamilton's father-in-law) and all its members shared Hamilton's political views. In brief, the Committee was stacked.

President Washington then referred the bill to Thomas Jefferson (Secretary of State) and Edmund Randolph (Attorney General). Both found it to be unconstitutional. Jefferson's opinion on the unconstitutionality of the bank included the following powerful argument:

I consider the foundation of the Constitution as laid on this ground; that "all powers not delegated to the United States by the Constitution nor prohibited by it to the states, are reserved to the states, or to the people."

To take a single step beyond the boundaries thus specifically drawn around the powers of Congress is to take possession of a boundless field of power no longer susceptible of any definition.

The Bill delivers us up bound to the National Bank, who are free to refuse all arrangements, but on their own terms, and the public not free, on such refusal, to employ any other bank. (5)

The Bank of New York

This was not Alexander Hamilton's first proposal for a self-interested bank charter: five years earlier, in 1784, Hamilton joined with Isaac Roosevelt and others to create the Bank of New York.

It is remarkable that academics have not emphasized the association of the Roosevelt family with the Bank of New York, the first bank founded in New York City and New York State and also one of the very first banks founded in the United States. Only the Bank of North America and the Pennsylvania Bank organized during the Revolutionary War preceded the Bank of New York.

The initial meeting of the Bank of New York was held March 15, 1784 and the following directors were present:[6]

Alexander McDougal (President)
Samuel Franklin
Robert Bowne
Comfort Sands
Alexander Hamilton
Joshua Waddington
Thomas B. Stoughton

William Maxwell
Nicholas Low
Daniel McCormick
Isaac Roosevelt
John Vanderbilt
Thomas Randall

Alexander Hamilton, who as we have seen, staunchly opposed Thomas Jefferson and the Jeffersonian democratic tradition in American politics, was connected with the Bank of New York from the start. The constitution of the Bank of New York was in fact written by Alexander Hamilton. And as most of the newly elected officers of the bank were not familiar with banking business it was Alexander Hamilton who provided a letter of introduction to the Bank of North America which supplied the necessary information and guidance.

The first president of the Bank of New York was Jeremiah Wadsworth. His tenure was brief and in May, 1786 Isaac Roosevelt was elected president, with William Maxwell as vice president. The bank offices were in the old Walton House with the Roosevelt sugar refinery just across the street at number 159 Quinn Street.

Conflict of interest is more than obvious on the part of Alexander Hamilton, who became Secretary of the Treasury when the Constitution of the United States went into effect in 1789. While Hamilton did not take a daily active part as director of the Bank of New York, Hamilton advised its cashier William Seaton, and in 1790 the bank of New York was made an agent of the United States government for the sale of *200,000 guilders*. Simultaneously Hamilton laid before Congress the idea of the Bank of the United States -a private banking monopoly.

Furthermore Hamilton used his cabinet influence to prevent the Bank of the United States from establishing a branch in the City of New York, in competition with the Bank of New York.

It also appears that Hamilton tried to make the Bank of New York the exclusive agent of the United States government in New York. In January, 1791 Alexander Hamilton wrote to William Seaton as follows:

I shall labor to give what has taken place a turn favorable to another union the propriety of which is to say clearly illustrated by the present state of things. It is my wish that the Bank of New York may by all means continue to receive deposits from the collection in the paper of the Bank of the United States and that they may also receive payment for the Dutch bills in the same paper.[7]

Later in the same letter, Hamilton writes as follows:

Be confidential with me if you are pressed whatever support may be in my power shall be afforded. I consider the public interest as materially involved in aiding a valuable institution like yours to withstand the attacks of a confederated host of frantic and I fear in too many instances unprincipled gamblers.

Alexander Hamilton was also overly protective when in 1791 a rival bank was proposed for New York City. When Hamilton heard of the project he expressed strong disapproval in a letter to William Seaton dated January 18, 1791:

I have learned with infinite pain the circumstance of a new bank having started up in your city. Its effects cannot but be in every way pernicious. I sincerely hope that the Bank of New York will listen to no coalition with this newly engendered monster, a better alliance I am strongly persuaded will be brought about for it and the joint force of two solid institutions will without effort or violence remove the excrescence just appeared. I express myself in these strong terms to you confidentially not that I have any objection to my opinion in being known as to the natural tendency of the thing.[8]

According to Myers' *History of the Great American Fortunes*[9] the

Bank of New York "injected itself virulently into politics and fought the spread of democratic ideas with sordid but effective weapons." It is Myers' contention that the bank and its founders in the Hamiltonian tradition fully understood the danger to their financial interests in the Jeffersonian principle.

Even in 1930 the Bank of New York contained a representative of the Roosevelt interests - W. Emlen Roosevelt was on the 1930 board as was Cleveland Dodge, the backer of Woodrow Wilson for president (see below), and Allen Wardwell, the J.P. Morgan partner influential in the Bolshevik Revolution of 1917.[10]

The Second Bank of the United States

On March 4, 1809 James Madison, a quiet, unassuming man, entered the office of President. In 1776 Madison was a member of the Virginia Convention and served on the committee which framed the Constitution and the Bill of Rights. In 1787 Madison became a member of the Virginia delegation to the Philadelphia Convention and made specific constitutional suggestions, assembled in the so-called 'Virginia Plan." In many ways Madison can be termed the "master builder of the Constitution." Consequently Madison's views on the constitutionality of private banking monopolies are fundamental. The charter of the First Bank expired in 1811 and Congress refused to grant a new charter on the grounds of unconstitutionality. President Madison's message repeated the argument on the unconstitutionality of the bank and made the following comment:

On the whole it is considered that the proposed establishments will:

1. enjoy a monopoly of the profits of a National Bank for a period of twenty years;

2. that the monopolized profits will be continually growing with the progress of the national population and wealth;

3. and that the nation will, during the same period, be dependent on the notes of the bank for the species of circulating medium whenever the precious metals may be wanted; and

4. at all times (will the nation be dependent on the notes of the bank) for so much thereof as may be an eligible substitute for a specie medium; and

5.   that the extensive employment of the notes (bank) in the collection of the augmented taxes will, moreover, enable the banks greatly to extend its profitable issues of them (bank notes) without the expense of specie capital to support their circulation;

It is as reasonable as it is requisite that the government, in return for these extraordinary concessions to the bank, should have a greater security for attaining the public objects of the institution than is presented in this Bill.... (11)

The War of 1812 presented bank supporters with a new argument - financial distress brought about by the war required financial relief in the form of a new national bank.

Under these pressing circumstances the House and Senate passed a bill creating the Second Bank of the United States. James Madison signed the bill into law April 10, 1816.

The Money Trust Honors Woodrow Wilson

Federal Reserve Notes have a curious matchup of denominations with Presidents. The highest value Federal Reserve Note of $100,000 bears the portrait of Woodrow Wilson, a real friend of the money trust. The next highest value of $10,000 bears the portrait of Samuel Chase, Lincoln's Treasury Secretary who pushed through the National Bank bill for the money interest.

Ben Franklin gets the $100 bill and Abe Lincoln the $5.00 bill. The only note in the 1934 Series that bears the inscription "payable in gold" is the

$100,000 note which is only used for transfers between the various Federal Reserve regional banks.

100,000
A00020113A
100,000
WASHINGTON, D.C.
THE UNITED STATES OF AMERICA
ONE HUNDRED THOUSAND DOLLARS IN GOLD

FEDERAL RESERVE NOTE
THE UNITED STATES OF AMERICA
100
THIS NOTE IS LEGAL TENDER FOR ALL DEBTS, PUBLIC AND PRIVATE
J00343826A
WASHINGTON, D.C.
J00343826A
ONE HUNDRED DOLLARS

FEDERAL RESERVE NOTE
THE UNITED STATES OF AMERICA
10,000
★00000000★
B
★00000000★
WASHINGTON, D.C.
WILL PAY TO THE BEARER ON DEMAND
TEN THOUSAND DOLLARS

FEDERAL RESERVE NOTE
THE UNITED STATES OF AMERICA
THIS NOTE IS LEGAL TENDER FOR ALL DEBTS, PUBLIC AND PRIVATE
F 85564589 F
WASHINGTON, D.C.
F
F 85564589 F
FIVE DOLLARS

Endnotes to Chapter Two

(1) The Writings of Jefferson, vol. 7 (Autobiography, Correspondence, Reports, Messages, Addresses and other Writings) (Committee of Congress: Washington, D.C., 1861) p. 685.

(2) *The History of the Constitution of the United States,* (D. Appleton & Co., New York, 1893) p. 31.

(3) Gaillard Hunt, *Writings of James Madison,* (Geo. P. Putnam's Sons, New York) vol. 6, p. 371.

(4) *Journal of Wm. McClay, United States Senator from Pennsylvania, 1789.* Edited by Edgar S. McClay, (D. Appleton & Co., New York, 1890) p. 371.

(5) *The Writings of Jefferson,* vol. 7, Joint Committee of Congress, *op cit.*

(6) Henry W. Dommett, *Bank of New York 1784-1884,* (Putnam's Sons, New York, 1884) p. 9.

(7) H. W. Dommett, *op. cit,* p. 41.

(8) *Ibid.,* p. 43.

(9) *Ibid.,* p. 125.

(10) Antony Sutton, *Wall Street and the Bolshevik Revolution,* (New York, Arlington House, 1974).

(11) Gaillard Hunt, *The Life and Writings of James Madison,* (New York, Putnam's Sons, 1908), vol. 8, p. 327.

Chapter Three

ANDREW JACKSON: THE LAST ANTI-ELITIST PRESIDENT

The original charter for the Second Bank of the United States was limited in time, unlike the present Federal Reserve System. A new charter for the (Second) Bank of the United States to replace the expiring grant was passed by Congress in July 1832, and President Andrew Jackson promptly vetoed the charter, with an emphatic message of major historical interest.

According to modern academic opinion the Jackson veto is "legalistic, demagogic and full of sham."[1] In fact, on reading the message today Andrew Jackson was clearly prophetic in his warnings and arguments to the American people. In the first inaugural address in January 1832, Jackson stated his position on the bank and renewal of the charter:

> As the Charter of the Bank of the United States will expire in 1836, and its stockholders will most probably apply for a renewal of their privileges; in order to avoid the evils resulting from precipitancy in a measure involving such important principles and such deep pecuniary interests, I feel that I cannot in justice to our constituents and to the parties interested too soon present it to the deliberate consideration of the Legislature and the people.
>
> The constitutionality of this law has been well questioned...because it grants to those who hold stock exclusive privileges of a dangerous tendency. Its expediency is denied by a large portion of our citizens...and it is believed none will deny that it has failed in the great end of our establishing a uniform and sound currency throughout the United States.[2]

Andrew Jackson's personal view on the Second Bank of the United States is contained in a memorandum in Jackson's own handwriting written in January, 1832.[3]

The opinion shows how far present constitutional interpretation has diverged from the intent of our founding fathers. Jackson's opening argument is that all "sovereign power is in the people and the states," and then argues that in cases, such as the power to grant corporations, where the power is not expressly given to the general (Federal) government, then "no sovereign power not expressly granted can be exercised, by implication." The key is "implied power." There are no implied powers in the Constitution.

Jackson goes on to argue that it may be possible for "necessity" to give power to grant charters to banks and corporations, but this must be a "positive necessity not a fained one." And then only within the ten mile square of Washington, DC itself does Congress have such sovereign power. Jackson argues as follows:

> *It is inconsistent with any of the powers granted that our government should form a corporation and become a member of it. The founders were too well aware of the corrupting influence of a great moneyed monopoly upon government to legalize such a corrupting monster by any grant either expressed or implied in the Constitution.*

The extraordinary difficulty and massive political power that Jackson faced in fighting the "money monopoly" and its influence is shown in his letter to Hugh L. White, dated April 29, 1831 (Vol. 4, page 271):

> *The great principles of democracy which we have both at heart to see restored to the federal government cannot be accomplished unless by a united cabinet who labor to this end. The struggles against the rechartering of the United States Bank are to be met. The corrupting influence of the Bank upon the morals of the people and upon Congress are to be fearlessly met....*
>
> *Many who you would not have supposed have secretly enlisted in its ranks and between bank men nullifiers and internal improvement men it is hard to get a cabinet who will unite with me heart and hand in the great task of democratic reform in the administration of our government.*[4]

By 1833 the struggle over the rechartering of the Bank of the United States had degenerated into a conflict between Andrew Jackson and his secretary of the treasury, William J. Duane and ultimately led to dismissal of Duane. Jackson wanted to withdraw all government deposits from the private Bank of the United States while Duane refused to order removal of the deposits.

In a letter dated June 26, 1833 (Vol. 5, page 111) Andrew Jackson expands on his demand for withdrawal of government deposits from the Bank of the United States, and proposes that one bank be selected in each of various cities to receive government deposits. State banks with good credit would be preferable to the concentration of government funds in one bank which was a private monopoly.

The letter was accompanied by a paper explaining Jackson's views on possible government relations with the Bank of the United States and the future. Included was this straightforward statement:

> *The framers (of our Constitution) were too well aware of the corrupting influences of a great moneyed monopoly upon government to legalize such a corrupting monster by any grant either express or implied in the constitution.*
>
> *Bank corporations are brokers on a large scale, and could it be really urged that the framers of the Constitution intended that our Government should become a Government of Brokers? If so, then the profits of the National Brokers Shop must enure to the benefit of the whole people, and not a few privileged moneyed capitalists, to the utter rejection of the many.*[5]

The opinion recalled that in December 1831 Congress petitioned for a renewal of the bank charter and Jackson had vetoed the bill. As Jackson was then a candidate for reelection this in effect brought the veto directly before the electorate and in approving the president the public also condemned the bill as both "inexpedient and unconstitutional."

In other words Jackson argued that his veto had already received public approval. Therefore, Jackson continued, "the duty of the bank was to wind up its concerns in such a manner that will produce the least pressure upon the money market."

Jackson recalled the extraordinary and rapid increase of government debt to the bank which had grown by $28 million or 66 percent in a period of 16 months. Jackson commented as follows:

> *The motive of the enormous extension of loans can no longer be doubted. It was unquestionably to gain power in the country and force the government through the influence of the debtors to grant it a new charter.*

This must be the first and last statement from an American President declaring what many now suspect: that certain banks (but not all bankers) use debt as a political weapon for control. We cannot include all bankers because bankers in Catholic countries, for example, are forbidden on grounds of religion from using debt for control. This would amount to usury.

Jackson goes on to outline the reasons for his wish to sever connections between the bank and the government:

a leading objection is that the Bank of the United States has the power and in that event will have the disposition to crush the state banks particularly those which may be selected by the government as the depositories of its funds and thus cause wide spread distress and ruin throughout the United States.

Then Jackson makes an argument strange to the ears of those reading in the 20th century:

The only currency known to the Constitution of the United States is gold and silver. This is consequently the only currency which that instrument delegates to Congress the power to regulate.

This suggests that Andrew Jackson would have considered the present Federal Reserve System, a private bank-owned monopoly, to be unconstitutional and in fact "the money monster" in new form.

President Andrew Jackson's final message on March 4, 1837 was unbelievably prophetic in its content - and the last time an American President was sufficiently independent of the elitist powers behind the scenes to publicly warn American citizens of the dangers to their freedoms and livelihood. Here is an extract from Jackson's final message to the American people:

The distress and alarm which pervaded and agitated the whole country when the Bank of the United States waged war upon the people in order to compel them to submit to its demands cannot yet be forgotten. The ruthless and unsparing temper with which whole cities and communities were oppressed, individuals impoverished and ruined, and a scene of cheerful prosperity suddenly changed into one of gloom and despondency ought to be indelibly impressed on the memory of the people of the United States.

If such was its power in a time of peace, what would it not have been in a season of war, with an enemy at your doors? No nation but the freemen of the United States could have come out victorious from such a contest; yet, if you had not conquered, the government would have passed from the hands of the many to the few, and this organized money power, from its secret conclave, would have dictated the choice of your highest officials and compelled you to make peace or war, as best suited their own wishes. [6]

Even while Jackson wrote this message to the American people our government had passed "from the hands of the many to the hands of the few." Moreover, the few "from its secret enclave" was already dictating political choices, boom and slump and war and peace.

In the United States the Jacksonian Democrats, the Whig tradition in American politics, were the last remnant that knew and understood the power behind the scenes. Across the Atlantic in England the Cobdenites under Richard Cobden and John Bright tried to maintain a similar torch of individual freedom. They also failed.

As Jackson wrote his last message, socialist manifestos were being weighed and put to paper. Not to improve the lot of the common man as they would have us believe, but as devices to gain political power for the elite.

Endnotes to Chapter Three

(1) Bray Hammond, *Banks and Politics in America,* (Princeton University Press, Princeton, 1957) p. 405. It is noteworthy that Princeton, one of the Ivy League schools, is a scholastic base of the "establishment" and helps perpetuate this one sided historical interpretation.

(2) James A. Hamilton, *Reminiscences,* p. 149.

(3) John Spencer Bassett, ed., *Correspondence of Andrew Jackson,* (Carnegie Institution, Washington, D.C., 1929-32) vol. 4, p. 389.

(4) *Ibid.,* p. 271. Jackson was not a skilled writer. He was a man of action and principle rather than a man of letters. However, his points are clearly there for those with eyes to read.

(5) *Ibid.,* p. 92.

(6) *Richardson's Messages,* Vol. 4, p. 1523.

Chapter Four

ROOSEVELT'S SOCIALIST MANIFESTO

The forces of "the few," i.e., the establishment elite, have been in the ascendancy since Jackson's last message of 1837. President Martin Van Buren tried briefly and failed to stem their power. Abraham Lincoln tried, and also failed. Every president since Lincoln has neglected even to try to curb the power of the elite.

On the one hand is the "money monopoly" controlling the status quo and the ruling establishments. On the other hand is the "revolution of rising expectations" superficially created by socialist revolutionaries, but in fact socialism in theory and practice is created, supported and controlled with debt and political power created by the "money monopoly."

In this chapter we will look at an American socialist manifesto, the forerunner of FDR's New Deal, written by Clinton Roosevelt in 1841. Clinton Roosevelt, one of the lesser known Roosevelt cousins was descended from the New York banking Roosevelts and linked by his socialist writings to the 20th century Roosevelts. Then in Chapter Five we will describe a more well-known manifesto, that of Karl Marx, also financed from the United States.

The "money monopoly" creates and nurtures socialism. Let's start to probe this idea with the Roosevelts, who have been both bankers and socialists simultaneously.

While one branch of the Roosevelt family developed the Bank of New York and the sugar refining industry, another branch of the family worked its way into practical politics and even theoretical political philosophy.

For example, long before Franklin Delano Roosevelt became President, James J. Roosevelt was a member of the New York State Legislature in 1835, 1839, and 1840, a member of the Loco Focos and distinguished himself by opposition to Whig attempts to eliminate "ballot stuffing."[1]

Roosevelt was not only powerful within Tammany Hall's inner

circle but according to one biographer, "he was in effect liaison officer between the Hall and Wall Street, one who carried orders from the bankers to the politicians and dictated nominations and elections in a ruthless manner."(2)

James Roosevelt was the 1840s link between the inner circles of Tammany Hall and Wall Street banking including the Roosevelts' own Bank of New York. But it was Clinton Roosevelt, born in 1804, son of Elbert Cornelius Roosevelt, who provided a socialist manifesto some years before Marx plagiarized his more famous Communist Manifesto from French Socialist Victor Considerant (see Chapter Five).

Clinton Roosevelt was a 19th-century cousin to Franklin Delano Roosevelt, and incidentally also related to President Theodore Roosevelt, John Quincy Adams, and President Martin Van Buren. Clinton Roosevelt's only literary effort is contained in a rare booklet dated 1841.(3) In essence it is a Socratic discussion between the author Roosevelt (i.e., the few) and a "Producer" presumably representing the rest of us (i.e., the many).

Roosevelt proposes a totalitarian government much like Karl Marx's, where all individuality is submerged to a collective run by an elitist aristocratic group (i.e., the few, or the vanguard in Marxist terms) who design and enact all legislation. Roosevelt demanded abandonment of the Constitution to achieve his goals:

> *P. (Producer): But I ask again: Would you at once abandon the old doctrines of the Constitution?*
>
> *A. (Author): Not by any means. Not any more than if one were in a leaky vessel he should spring overboard to save himself from drowning. It is a ship put hastily together when we left the British flag, and it was then thought an experiment of very doubtful issue.(4)*

The Rooseveltian system depended "First, on the art and science of cooperation. This is to bring the whole to bear for our mutual advantage." It is this cooperation, i.e., the ability to bring the whole to bear for the interest of the few, that is the encompassing theme of writings and preachings from Marx to the present Trilateral Commission. In the Roosevelt schema each man rises through fixed and specified grades in the social system and is appointed to a class of work to which he is best suited. Choice of occupation is strictly limited. In the words of Clinton Roosevelt:

Whose duty will it be to make appointments to each class?

A. The Grand Marshal's.

P. Who will be accountable that the men appointed are the best qualified?

A. A Court of physiologists, Moral Philosophers, and Farmers and Mechanics, to be chosen by the Grand Marshal and accountable to him.

P. Would you constrain a citizen to submit to their decisions in the selection of a calling?

A. No. If any one of good character insisted, he might try until he found the occupation most congenial to his tastes and feelings. (5)

Then Roosevelt invented the Marshal of Creation, whose job it is to balance production and consumption, much like a master planner:

P. What is the duty of the Marshal of the Creating or Producing order?

A. It is to estimate the amount of produce and manufactures necessary to produce a sufficiency in each department below him. When in operation, he shall report excesses and deficiencies to the Grand Marshal.

P. How shall he discover such excesses and deficiencies?

A. The various merchants will report to him the demand and supplies in every line of business, as will be seen hereafter.

P. Under this order are agriculture, manufactures and commerce, as I perceive. What then is the duty of the Marshal of Agriculture?

A. He should have under him four regions, or if not, foreign commerce must make good the deficiency.

P. What four regions?

A. The temperate, the warm, the hot region and the water region.

P. Why divide them thus?

A. Because the products of these different regions require different systems of cultivation, and are properly subject to different minds.⁽⁶⁾

Seventy-five years later, in 1915, Bernard Baruch was invited by President Woodrow Wilson to design a plan for a defense mobilization committee. This Baruch plan subsequently became the War Industries Board, which absorbed and replaced the old General Munitions Board. The War Industries Board as a concept was similar to cooperative trade associations, a device long desired by Wall Street to control the unwanted rigors of competition in the marketplace, and much like Clinton Roosevelt's 1841 Plan. Committees of industry, big business and small business, both represented in Washington, and both with Washington representation back home ... this was to be the backbone of the whole structure.

By March, 1918, President Wilson, acting without Congressional authority, had endowed Baruch with more power than any other individual had been granted in the history of the United States. The War Industries Board, with Baruch as its chairman, became responsible for building all factories and for the supply of all raw material, all products, and all transportation, and all its final decisions rested with chairman Baruch.

The War Industries Board was the organizational forerunner of the 1933 National Recovery Administration and some of the 1918 WIB corporate elite appointed by Baruch - Hugh Johnson, for example - found administrative niches in Roosevelt's NRA Plan. Comparison of Roosevelt's New Deal, actually written by Gerard Swope of General Electric, with Clinton Roosevelt's early 1841 scheme shows a remarkable similarity.

Clinton Roosevelt - The Science of Government
(New York 1841)

This is a proposal for a totalitarian government without individual rights run by an elitist establishment. Clinton Roosevelt was a cousin of Franklin Delano Roosevelt. The book has been removed from the current Library of Congress catalog although it was listed in the earlier 1959 edition.

THE SCIENCE OF GOVERNMENT,

FOUNDED ON

NATURAL LAW.

BY

CLINTON ROOSEVELT.

NEW YORK:
PUBLISHED BY DEAN & TREVETT,
121 FULTON STREET.
1841.

Endnotes to Chapter Four

(1) Karl Schriftgiesser, *The Amazing Roosevelt Family, 1613-1942* (New York: Wilfred Funk, 1942) p. 143.

(2) *Ibid., p.* 142. Examination of the charts on pages xi and xii of Schriftgiesser show that Franklin Delano Roosevelt, the so-called anti-bank candidate in 1932, also descends in direct line from New York Bank founder Isaac Roosevelt.

(3) Clinton Roosevelt, *The Science of Government Founded on Natural Law* (New York: Dean & Trevett, 1841). There are two known copies of this book: one in the Library of Congress, Washington D.C. and another in the Harvard University Library. The existence of the book is censored (i.e., omitted) in the latest edition of the Library of Congress catalog, but was recorded in the earlier 1959 edition (page 75). A facsimile edition was published by Emanuel J. Josephson, as part of his *Roosevelt's Communist Manifesto* (New York: Chedney Press, 1955).

(4) Ibid.

(5) Ibid.

(6) *Ibid.*

Chapter Five

KARL MARX AND HIS MANIFESTO

The modern welfare state such as we have in the United States has a remarkable resemblance to the Communist Manifesto supposedly written by Karl Marx in 1848. The ten points of the Marxian Manifesto, a program designed to overthrow the middle class bourgeoisie (not the big capitalists) have been implemented by successive Democrat and Republican governments since Woodrow Wilson under guidance of a self-perpetuating establishment.

Marx's big enemy was the middle class, the bourgeoisie. Marx wanted to seize property from this middle class in a revolution led by the so-called working class, or the proletariat. Unfortunately for Marx the working class has never had too much liking for communist revolution, as we saw in the Revolutions of the 1980s. In practice, communist revolution is led by a handful of communists. How can a revolution be made and kept in power by a small group? Only because communists have always had help from the so-called ruling class - capitalists and bankers. This aid and assistance has been consistent from financing Marx's Manifesto in 1848 down to the late 20th century when a David Rockefeller-dominated Administration is helping Communist revolution and revolutionaries in Central America, Angola and Mozambique.

Let's start with the 1848 Manifesto. Marx wanted to seize middle class property. In the Manifesto, Marx phrased the objective like this:

> In the first instance, of course, this can only be effected by despotic interference with bourgeois methods of production; that is to say by measures which seem economically inadequate and untenable, but have far-reaching effects, and are necessary as means for revolutionizing the whole system of production.[1]

To bring about this "despotic" seizure of middle class property, Marx laid out a ten-point program of "measures" as follows:

> These measures will naturally differ from country to country. In

the most advanced countries they will, generally speaking, take the following forms:

1. *Expropriation of landed property, and the use of land rents to defray State expenditure.*
2. *A vigorously graduated income tax.*
3. *Abolition of the right of inheritance.*
4. *Confiscation of the property of all émigrés and rebels.*
5. *Centralisation of credit in the hands of the State, by means of a national bank with State capital and an exclusive monopoly.*
6. *Centralisation of the means of transport in the hands of the State.*
7. *Increase of national factories and means of production, cultivation of uncultivated land, and improvement of cultivated land in accordance with a general plan.*
8. *Universal and equal obligation to work; organization of industrial armies, especially for agriculture.*
9. *Agriculture and urban industry to work hand-in-hand, in such a way as, by degrees, to obliterate the distinction between town and country.*
10. *Public and free education of all children. Abolition of factory work for children in its present form. Education and material production to be combined.*[(2)]

As we shall see later, Marx's ten points for destruction of the middle class have almost been completed in the United States. The 16th Amendment, for example (the income tax) is an archaic political concept that goes back some 4,000 years in history to the time of the Pharaohs in Egypt.

The Pharaohs and their elitist advisors had the notion that the entrepreneur, the businessmen, and the workers of Egypt who produced the wealth of that civilization somehow were not competent to manage that wealth.

These elitist advisors and Pharaoh said, "Look, we're going to force you people to do what we know you should. Because after all, were omnipotent, we are standing up here looking down on all of you and we can decide what is best for all. Much better than each of you can individually decide for yourselves. We're going to force you to have a government retirement program, so that when you reach retirement age you can retire with some dignity. We're going to force you to do what we know you should do, because we know you won't do it if left to your own devices. Also, we're going to force you to have a government food storage program. We're going to store grain in the government granaries because we know that you are not competent - you are not capable of storing food by yourselves.

"Furthermore, we know you can't take care of your health so we're going to force you to have a government medical program. We know health is important and we know that you don't have the responsibility or capability for looking after yourselves. We're going to force it on you for your own best interests."

The method used to accomplish these objectives was to withhold a fifth part of the production of Egypt. If you go back and read the Old Testament it says, "That the Pharaoh had decided to take up a fifth power of the production of Egypt and to store it in granaries for the benefit of all."

The modern day proponent of the Pharaoh's philosophy is none other than Karl Marx and the Communist Manifesto. The Manifesto has become the most significant economic document of the 20th Century. The significance lies in the unfortunate fact that the Manifesto is the economic guiding light of our leadership today, of the executive branch of our government and in most cases the leadership of both parties in this country who work to support and bring about the measures of the manifesto.

Basically what the Manifesto states is that when you have implemented these 10 programs in any free enterprise system, "capitalism" will have been destroyed and a communist state established in its place. This is what Marx wrote:

> *Strictly speaking, political power is the organized use of force by one class in order to keep another class in subjection. When the proletariat, in the course of its fight against the bourgeoisie, necessarily consolidates itself into a class, by means of a revolution makes itself the ruling class, it forcibly sweeps away the old system of production.*

Item 2 of Marx's Manifesto reads as follows: *A heavy, progressive, or graduating income tax"*

This became the 16th Amendment of the United States Constitution, the law of the land in our country since 1913.

Later on in 1913 we saw the passage of the Federal Reserve Act. Interestingly enough the idea for that program is in Karl Marx's program in the Communist Manifesto as Item 5 and is possibly the most important point in the Communist Manifesto. Item 5 reads as follows: *Centralization of Credit in the hands of the state by means of a National Bank with state capital and exclusive monopoly.*

In other words Marx proposed a scheme exactly like the First Bank of the United States and the Federal Reserve Act with establishment of a fractional reserve central banking system on the model of the earlier European central banks.

Karl Marx as a Plagiarist

Marx was a brilliant fellow. He was no fool. Marx knew that if he could place under the control of a small group of men the ability to control the supply of money and credit of any nation, he could boom or bust those economies almost at will. By having foreknowledge of economic and monetary policies, billions of dollars of wealth could be transferred from one group to another, from the suffering middle class to the ruling elite. To do this required propaganda and in the mid-19th century the pamphlet was an effective means of propagandizing.

A most interesting feature of the brief Manifesto has been almost universally ignored by academics, i.e., that the Manifesto doesn't favor the working class at all and it certainly doesn't favor the middle class which is targeted for elimination.

The Manifesto is a blueprint for elitist control. The Manifesto favors takeover of political and economic power by an elite. And when we look at the source of the assistance given to Marx, it is clear that the benefits to the elite were obvious even in the 1840s.

Marx was certainly paid to write the Manifesto, as we shall see later. Furthermore, the Manifesto was plagiarized from an obscure French socialist named Victor Considerant, and his work, *Principes du Socialisme: Manifeste de la Democratie au Dix Neuvieme Siecle,* published in 1843. The second edition of Considerant's work was published in Paris in 1847, a year before the Manifesto and while Marx and Engels were living in Paris.

The plagiarism was spotted by an even more obscure writer, W. Tcherkesoff, and published in precise detail in his *Pages of Socialist History* (Cooper, New York, 1902).

the United States.

The conduit for financing the printing of the Manifesto was none other than Louisiana pirate Jean Laffite, who was, among his later occupations, a spy for Spain and a courier for a group of American bankers.

The evidence for this twist in modern history has been ignored by modern historians although the documents, authenticated by Library of Congress and other sources, have been available for some 30 years.

It is extraordinary that the first academics to report this source of financing for Marx were written in French, not English! It was a French book by Georges Blond entitled *Histoire de la Filibuste* that contains the remarkable story of Karl Marx as a friend of Jean Laffite the pirate who "financed the printing of the Manifesto of the Communist party." Where did Blond get his information? It originated in two privately printed books published in New Orleans by Stanley Clisby Arthur, *Jean Laffite, the Gentleman Rover* and *The Journal of Jean Laffite*. These books contain original documents describing meetings between Marx and Laffite and the method used to finance the Manifesto.

Now of course if you look up the name Jean Laffite in the *Encyclopedia Britannica*, you will learn that Laffite died in 1823 and therefore could not possibly have financed Marx in 1847 and 1848. Unfortunately the *Britannica* is wrong, as it is on many other points. Laffite went underground about 1820 and lived a long and exciting life as courier for American bankers and businessmen.

Laffite's courier and underground work for American bankers is noted in *The Journal*:

> *We employed four men as secret officers to spy and report every pertinent conversation and to make verbal reports about any new happenings. We carried out our secret missions very well. We had only two ships operating under private contract with banking interests in Philadelphia. We decided, and took our oath, never to visit saloons or travel the same route twice, or ever go back to Louisiana, Texas or Cuba or any of the Spanish speaking countries.*[4]

In the same Journal under date of April 24, 1848 we find the note:

> *My interviews were brief, but direct. I lived at the home of Mr. Louis Bertillon in Paris and sometimes hotels. I met Mr. Michel Chevreul, Mr. Louis Braille, Mr. Augustin Thierry, Mr. Alexis de*

Tocqueville, Mr. Karl Marx, Mr. Frederic Engels, Mr. Daguerre and many others. [5]

Then Laffite goes on to the eye-opening statement:

Nobody knew the real facts about my mission in Europe. I opened an account in a bank in Paris, a credit in escrow to finance two young men, Mr. Marx and Mr. Engels to help bring about the revolution of working men of the world. They are now working at it. [6]

So here we have it. Jean Laffite was the agent of American banking interests and arranged for the financing of the Manifesto. In *The Journal* the reader will find other prominent names, i.e., Dupont, Peabody, Lincoln and so on.

While Jean Laffite was in Brussels he wrote at length to his artist friend De Franca in St. Louis, Missouri about financing Marx. Here's the translation of the letter dated September 29, 1847:

I am leaving Brussels for Paris, in three or four weeks I will go to Amsterdam, then enroute for America. I have had a number of conversations with Mr. Marx and Mr. Engels, but have refused to participate in the conferences with the other debaters to compose the manifest, because I do not wish to be identified with the other men.

Mr. Engels is going with me to Paris so that I may prepare a schedule to finance Mr. Marx and him, for a long time in advance, to proceed with their manuscripts, and to put in texts "Capital and Labor." From the beginning it seemed to me that the two young men are themselves gifted and endowed, I firmly believe, with the highest intelligence and that they merit this is justified by the statistic research in the discovery on "La Categorie du Capital," Value, Price and Profit.

They have penetrated a forgotten time in the exploitation of man by man without halt. From the Serf, of the Feudal Slave, and the Salaried Slave, they discover that exploitation is at the base of all evil. It has taken a long time to prepare "The manifests for the workers of the world." A great debate took place between the two young men and others from Berlin, Amsterdam, Paris, and others from the Swiss Republic.

I am enthused in regard to the manifests and other prospects for the future, as I heartily support the two young men. I hope and I pray that the projects may become joined in a strong doctrine to shake the foundations of the highest dynasties and leave them to be devoured by the lower masses.

Mr. Marx advises and warns me not to plunge into all America with the manifests because there are others of the same kind for New York. But I hope that Jean or Harry will show the manifests to Mr. Joshua Speed, and he, in his turn, can show them to Mr. Lincoln. I know that nothing else can confuse it, as it would have the same chance. Its reception at Washington would be a sacred promise that the path that I am on is in conformity with the policy at present pursued in the Republic of Texas.

Mr. Marx accepts some of my texts on the communes that I was forced to abandon some time ago, weighing carefully rules and regulations not based on a strong foundation, as so-called pure and simple Utopia, without preamble or body, without an apparent base to build on. I was in accord with the two young men at this date, apropos of my Utopian dreams of the past.

The sacrifice was made to preserve the great manuscript that was composed and its constitution, to endure forever with the radiance of the stars, but not for those in power to abuse or exploit.

Oh! to my dismay; I have agreed to the abuses practiced in the last part of the same year after the Dragon was eradicated and utterly abolished. I have described my second commune which I was forced to break up and abandon to the flambeau March 3, 1821, I then took the resolution to withdraw without convert. I am no longer aiding those who are opposed to my principles.

I must stop. I will bring several manuscripts and the manifest. I hope that Jules and Glenn are progressing at school with Miss Wing and Miss Burgess. I know they have much patience as teachers. Glenn is not as strong as Jules.[6]

The second source of American financing for Karl Marx came from Charles Anderson Dana, Editor of the New York Tribune owned by Horace Greeley. Both Dana and Greeley were fraternally associated with the Clinton Roosevelt we cited in Chapter Three and with his Roosevelt Manifesto for dictatorial government. Dana hired Marx to write for the New York Tribune. This Marx did, in over 500 articles spread over ten years from 1851 to 1861.

Marx's prime source of German funds came from his associate

Frederic Engels, son of a wealthy Bremen cotton manufacturer and subsidy provider to Marx for many years.

More surprising is the subsidy to Marx from the Prussian elite. Karl Marx married Jenny von Westphalen. Jennys brother Baron Ferdinand von Westphalen was Minister of the Interior in Prussia (overseeing the police department) while Karl was under "investigation" by this same Prussian department.

In other words, Marx's brother-in-law was in charge of investigating subversive activities. Over the years the von Westphalen family strongly supported Marx. For 40 years the Marx's maid, Demuth, was paid by the Westphalens and in fact Demuth was personally selected for the job by Baroness Caroline von Westphalen. Two of Karl Marx's early essays were actually written in the von Westphalen estate at Kreuznach, and money from the estate was left to Marx.

In brief, between the American bankers and the German aristocracy Marx was well funded for the Manifesto and later writings. Why would the elite fund Marx? Simply because the entire Marxist philosophical battery is aimed at extermination of the middle class and the supremacy of the elite. Marxism is a device for consolidating power by the elite. It has nothing to do with relieving the misery of the poor or advancing mankind: it is an elitist political device pure and simple.

Endnotes to Chapter Five

(1) Ryazinsky, *Communist Manifesto,* (New York: Russell & Russell, Inc., 1963) p. 52.

(2) *Op. Cit.*

(3) W. Tcherkesoff, *Pages of Socialist History,* p. 56

(4) *The Journal of Jean Laffite* (The Pirateer - Patriot's own story) (Vantage Press, New York, 1958) p. 126

(5) *Op. Cit.* p. 132-33

(6) *Ibid.*

(7) From the translation in Stanley C. Arthur's *Jean Laffite, Gentleman Rover* (Harmanson, New Orleans, 1952) pp. 262 and 265.

Chapter Six

ABRAHAM LINCOLN: LAST PRESIDENT TO FIGHT THE MONEY POWER

Abraham Lincoln was the last of several populist presidents to fight against the money monopoly. Lincoln from the very beginning of his Administration faced a heavy burden of financing the Civil War with a monetary system under private control. During the Civil War the Union government was hard-pressed to raise sufficient funds to pay troops, there was a shortage of coin and the private banking system was unwilling to meet the needs of the Union Army without personal gain.

Lincoln was in the Jeffersonian-Jacksonian tradition. This tradition reserved the right to issue currency to the Federal Government and argued that this right could not lawfully be transferred to a private monopoly. In 1862 Lincoln presented to Congress a bill to make United States notes full legal tender and so enable the Federal Government to print sufficient paper money to finance the Civil War. Presumably while Lincoln did not envisage the inflationary potential in expanding the government's spending power there is little question that his financial program was intended as a means of paying off debts and government expense without allowing the private money monopoly to profit from the public purse.

Unfortunately, Lincoln's Secretary of the Treasury, Samuel Portland Chase, was an ally of the banking interests. During the Civil War Chase supported Lincoln's monetary policy but later presented legislation to Congress favorable to the banking interests. Similarly Senator John Sherman, responsible for Senate passage of financial legislation, added even more financial power to that already granted the money monopoly in the form of National Bank legislation.

Lincoln's legal tender bill was reported on February 25, 1862. This was to issue $150 million of legal tender United States notes. At that time Secretary Chase commented:

> *I have a greater aversion to making anything but coin a legal tender in payment of debt;...it is however at present*

impossible in consequence of the large expenditure entailed by the war to procure sufficient coin for disbursements: And it has therefore become indispensably necessary that we should resort to the issue of United States notes. (1)

In similar manner Senator John Sherman of Ohio advocated the measure on the grounds, "in no other way could the payment of the troops and the satisfaction of other just demands be so economically or so well provided for."

However this program of a national currency was opposed by the New York banking interests and Senator John Sherman's advocation did not, as we shall see later, reflect his true intent. (To be repeated in 1913 by Senator Owen and Congressman Glass who misrepresented their true positions to the public on the Federal Reserve Act.)

The idea of a national currency was opposed by banking interests, the money power, because it would obviously remove from bankers the privilege of issuing an effective substitute for money (defined in the Constitution as gold and silver). What bankers wanted the government to undertake was transfer the right to issue money to banking interests, i.e., to allow bankers to act as agents of the Federal Government. The U.S. Government would then be a perpetual borrower required to borrow funds at interest from a private money monopoly - which had obtained the monopoly power from the government itself. Given the restrictions of the Constitution, banking interests had to tread carefully.

The Clinton Roosevelt (Bank of New York) proposal was to remove the Constitution, shadowed in the late 20th century by the Trilateral Commission pleas that the Constitution is outdated.

Moreover the public itself, apart from Constitutional limits, would hardly agree to a private money monopoly if the truth were to be widely known. So we find from the time of Jefferson to the 1990s that any discussion of a private money monopoly is quickly and thoroughly suppressed. *Nothing is more dangerous to the power of the elite than the public discovery and understanding of the private control of money supply.*

What the bankers wanted in the 1860s was for the government to issue interest-bearing bonds. These bonds were to be used as the basis of bank credit. While Lincoln pushed his legal tender act the bankers met to draft what became the National Bank Act of 1863.

The purpose of the National Bank Act was to give control of the money issue to bankers. This monopoly could be used for profit and with the Civil War, profits would be substantial.

The difference between Lincoln and the money power was essentially whether the medium of exchange (convertible bank notes and inconvertible bank credit transferred by check) was to be created and issued by private monopoly or government monopoly. In other words, whether the power of government is subordinate to a banking elite or bankers subject to the power of government which, if Congress did its job honestly, also means subordinate to the power of the people.

An extraordinary letter from Senator John Sherman to Rothschild Brothers in London dated June 25, 1863 (and leaked on Wall Street in 1863) demonstrates the double dealing of even "prominent" and "well regarded" politicians.

Sherman saw a chance to curry favor with the preeminent world bankers of the time and personally brought the possibilities of the proposed National Banking Act to the attention of international bankers. On the following pages we reproduce a letter from Rothschild Brothers (London) to Ikleheimer, Morton and Vandergould (Wall Street, New York) acknowledging receipt of a Sherman letter and relaying its contents. These bankers reply to Rothschild Brothers on July 6, 1863, with details of the National Banking Act and some insights into the character of Senator John Sherman.

London, June 25, 1863;
Messrs. Ikleheimer, Morton and Vandergould
No. 3, Wall St.,
New York, U.S.A.

Dear Sirs:

A Mr. John Sherman has written us from a town in Ohio, U.S.A., as to the profit that may be made in the National Banking business, under a recent act of your Congress; a copy of this act accompanies this letter.

Apparently this act has been drawn up on the plan formulated here by the British Bankers Association, and by that Association recommended to our American friends, as one that if enacted into law, would prove highly profitable to the banking fraternity throughout the world.

Mr. Sherman declares that there has never been such an opportunity for capitalists to accumulate money as that presented by this act. It gives the National Bank almost complete control of the National finance. "The few who understand the system," he says, "will either be so interested in its profits, or so dependent on its favors that there will be no opposition from that class, while on the other hand, the great body of people, mentally incapable of comprehending the tremendous advantages that Capital derives from the system, will bear its burden without complaint, and perhaps without even suspecting that the system is inimical to their interests....

Your respectful servants
Rothschild Brothers

New York City
July 6, 1863
Messrs. Rothschild Brothers,
London, England.
Dear Sirs:

We beg to acknowledge receipt of your letter of June 25, in which you refer to a communication received of Honorable John Sherman of Ohio, with reference to the advantages and profits of an American investment under the provisions of the National Banking Act.

Mr. Sherman possesses in a marked degree the distinguishing characteristics of a successful financier. His temperament is such that whatever his feelings may be they never cause him to lose sight of the main chance.

He is young, shrewd and ambitious. He has fixed his eyes upon the Presidency of the United States and is already a member of Congress (he has financial ambitions, too). He rightfully thinks that he has everything to gain by being friendly with men and institutions having large financial resources, and which at times are not too particular in their methods, either of obtaining government aid, or protecting themselves against unfriendly legislation.

As to the organization of the National Bank here and the nature and profits of such investment we beg leave to refer to our printed circulars enclosed herein, vis:

"Any number of persons not less than five may organize a National Banking Corporation.

"Except in cities having 6000 inhabitants or less, a National Bank cannot have less than $1,000,000 capital.

"They are private corporations organized for private gain, and select their own officers and employees.

"They are not subject to control of State Laws, except as Congress may from time to time provide.

"They may receive deposits and loan the same for their own benefit. They can buy and sell bonds and discount paper and do a general banking business.

"To start a National Bank on the scale of $1,000,000 will require purchase of that amount (par value) of U. S. Government Bonds.

"U. S. Government Bonds can now be purchased at 50% discount, so that a bank of $1,000,000 capital can be started at this time for only $500,000.

"These bonds must be deposited in the U.S. Treasury at Washington as security for the National Bank currency, that will be furnished by the government to the bank.

"The United States Government will pay 6% interest on the bonds in gold, the interest being paid semi-annually. It will be seen that at the present price of bonds the interest paid by the government itself is 12% in gold on all money invested.

"The U.S. Government on having the bonds aforesaid deposited with the Treasurer, on the strength of such security will furnish National currency to the bank depositing the bonds, at an annual interest of only one per cent per annum.

"The currency is printed by the U.S. Government in a form so like greenbacks, that the people do not detect the difference although the currency is but a promise of the bank to pay.

"The demand for money is so great that this money can be readily loaned to the people across the counter of the bank at a discount at the rate of 10% at thirty to sixty days' time, making it about 12% interest on the currency.

"The interest on the bonds, plus the interest on the currency which the bonds secure, plus incidentals of the business, ought to make the gross earnings of the bank amount to from 28% to 33-1/3%.

"National Banks are privileged to increase and contract their currency at will and, of course, can grant or withhold loans as they may see fit. As the banks have a National organization and can easily act together in withholding loans or extending them, it follows that they can by united action in refusing to make loans cause a stringency in the money market, and in a single week or even a single day cause a decline in all products of the country.

"National Banks pay no taxes on their bonds, nor on their capital, nor on their deposits."

Requesting that you will regard this as strictly confidential....

Most respectfully yours,

Ikelheimer, Morton and Vandergould [3]

It was particularly important to international bankers that they succeed with Lincoln. If Lincoln implemented public control of finance in the United States then other nations would pluck up courage to strip financial power from their bankers.

European bankers, especially those in England, organized against Abraham Lincoln and used commercial banking channels to pressure bankers in the U.S. for support. The Legal Tender Bill wanted by Lincoln was subjected to intense lobbying in Washington and so loaded with amendments as to become useless. One amendment required that interest on bonds and notes - mere pieces of paper - was to be paid twice a year in gold coin. Suffocation by ridiculous amendments was successful. Defeat of the Legal Tender Bill was followed in 1862 by a bill to allow banks to issue private bank notes less than $5.00 within the District of Columbia, a first step towards a privately controlled fiat money supply.

On July 23, 1862 Lincoln vetoed the Private Bank Note Bill on grounds that it was the responsibility of the Federal Government to provide a circulating medium and that United States notes could equally fulfill the function of small private notes. This veto was Lincoln's challenge to the banking interests.

Lincoln was a caustic critic of bankers. A delegation of New York bankers came to Washington to lobby in favor of the Legal Tender Bill. The Secretary of the Treasury introduced the delegation as follows:

These gentlemen from New York have come to see the Secretary of the Treasury about our new loan. As bankers they are obliged to hold our national securities. I can vouch for their patriotism and loyalty, for, as the Good Book says, "for where the treasure is, there will the heart be also."

Lincoln replied: *There is another test that I might apply, "Wherever the carcass is, there will the eagles be gathered together."*[4];

Lincoln's national currency scheme was in direct opposition to the international bankers who at that time planned to extend the Bank of England gold standard private money to the United States. Later in the 20th century bankers went for fiat money not backed by gold but in the mid-19th century the gold-silver system offered more opportunities for personal gain.

Lincoln was proposing that instead of the Federal Government borrowing paper or created money from the bankers that the bankers borrow coin or gold from the Treasury. In this way the banking interest would be unable to create fictional wealth from the printing press.

The National Bank Act was presented to the United States as a device to raise money to run the Civil War and achieve financial stability. Under the Act any five persons could form a bank with a capital of $50,000 or more. After deposit in the United States Treasury of interest-bearing bonds equal to one-third of the paid-in capital, the Government would print National Bank certificates on behalf of the bank to the amount of 90 percent of the part value of the bonds printed.

These National Bank certificates could then be used by the bank to carry on banking business and receive full profit on them as though they were the bank's own notes. Furthermore the bank received from the Federal Government interest payments in gold coin on bonds deposited in the Treasury.

In other words the bankers had a double profit. First, interest on government guaranteed money issues and second, interest paid on bonds in gold. The National Banking Act was a guaranteed profit making machine for anyone who wanted to get into banking.

Once again the Jeffersonian-Jacksonian tradition raised its voice. It claimed that the National banking system would create an even greater centralization of the money power than the Bank of the United States - which Andrew Jackson had vetoed.

This time around the money power was much more organized. The National Banking Bill was in the Senate only three or four days and in the House only two days before it was rushed through at a particularly critical time in the Civil War. The Bill was signed into law by President Lincoln on February 25, 1863.

Endnotes to Chapter Six

(1) Letter from Secretary of the Treasury Chase to Elbridge, G. Spaulding, January 29, 1862. Quoted in *American Nation History Series, 1861-1863* by Hosmer, vol. 20, pg. 169.

(2) John R. Elsom, *Lightning Over the Treasury Building* (or an expose of our banking and currency monstrosity, Americas most reprehensible and un-American racket), (Boston: Meador Publishing Co., 1941), pp. 51-52.

(3) *Op. cit.* pp. 53-55.

(4) *Ibid.*

Chapter Seven

THE MONEY TRUST CREATES THE FED

How would you like to have the *Wall Street Journal* one week ahead of publication?

Some people do have this privilege, not advance issues of *Wall Street Journal;* but advance knowledge of Federal Reserve policies... what they will be tomorrow, next week, next month and next year.

From time to time the Fed makes pronouncements and before the pronouncement they have to decide what to pronounce. They get together, they discuss, they make plans and then they issue statements.

The meetings are always secret, known only to the Fed Directors. However, if *we* knew what Chairman Alan Greenspan was going to announce on monetary and credit policies, what the discount rate will be, or what the prime rate will be, we could quickly make a fortune, because that knowledge has impact on Treasury bill rates, on metals markets, on the stock market and on real estate markets.

The Federal Reserve System is a *private* system owned by the banks and gives only banks this advance information.

The idea for the Fed was conceived on a small island in the Atlantic Ocean off Glynn County, Georgia. Back in 1910 Jekyll Island was a private club used by an elitist group of Wall Street financiers as a hideaway to discuss extra private business away from prying public ears. It was on Jekyll Island that the money trust designed its plan for Congressional approval of a private money monopoly.

American public opinion at the turn of the century was hostile to the idea of a central bank and generally opposed any further power for Wall Street interests. Yet a central bank along European lines offered vast secure profits for any financial group that could persuade Congress to enact central bank legislation. An elastic fiat and credit system offered power not possible with gold and silver as rigid disciplines on the financial system.

The clandestine Jekyll Island meeting was to design a plan to bring a central bank to the United States disguised as a regional banking system....while the bankers publicly opposed what they privately proposed.

This dissimulation was so successful that, according to private secretary Joseph Tumulty, Woodrow Wilson, in signing the Federal Reserve Act actually believed he was removing financial power from Wall Street interests.

President Wilson when governor of New Jersey in 1911 had declared:

The greatest monopoly in this country is the money monopoly. So long as that exists, our old variety of freedom and individual energy of development are out of the question.

A great industrial nation is controlled by its system of credit. Our system of credit is concentrated. The growth of the nation, therefore, and all our activities are in the hands of a few men....

This is the greatest question of all: and to this statesmen must address themselves with earnest determination to serve the long future and the true liberties of free men.[1]

Wilson may actually have believed his own statement that the Federal Reserve System was "the keystone of the great arch of the Democratic Administration."[2] What then is the reality behind this financial power known 100 years ago as the "money trust" or the "money power" and today as an elite group that can profit from a central bank?

To answer this question we have to go back in history and look at the 19th century trusts and the financial tip of the trust pyramid as it existed in the first decade of the twentieth century.

Between 1870 and the onset of World War One, American industry was concentrated under the control or influence of a handful of financiers, mostly in New York. John Moody, editor of the standard reference, *Moody's Manual of Corporation Securities,* recorded the trustification of American industry in a monumental volume of statistics and evidence.[3] Moody was a sympathetic observer and like Clarence Barron[4] another acute observer, considered trusts to be both useful and inevitable.

Criticism of the industrial trusts was widespread. John Moody's *The Truth About Trusts* with its wealth of detail demonstrated the pervasive money powers dominating the steel, non-ferrous metals, oil, tobacco, shipping, sugar and railroad industries - specifically the power of J.P. Morgan, the Rockefeller brothers, Edward Harriman, John McCormick, Henry Havemeyer and Thomas F. Ryan.

In tracing the early history of the drive for an American central bank by the "money power," two historical episodes stand out:

(l) the 1907 financial panic used by the bankers and their allies to urge the necessity for a central bank (although the panic was precipitated by Wall Street, this was not proven until many years later.)

(2) the meteoric rise of German banker Paul Warburg with his missionary zeal to promote a carbon copy of the German Reichsbank in the United States.

In 1907 there were still a few capitalists willing to challenge Wall Street and dispute its iron grip on financial power. Among these outsiders was Montana copper millionaire Frederick Augustus Heinze, who was selected as the key target for the 1907 panic. Heinze brought his copper fortune to New York and joined with C. W. Morse of the Ice Trust. Jointly they acquired control of Mercantile National Bank, using the assets of the Bank of North America already dominated by Morse.

Heinze and Morse then acquired control of the Knickerbocker Trust Company, allied with the Trust Company of America and Lincoln Trust. They then incorporated a speculative vehicle, the United Copper Company. It was stock market games with United Copper that precipitated the 1907 crisis. Banks under control of the "money trust" called their loans to United Copper and began a run on the Heinze-Morse Mercantile National Bank. It is now generally agreed "that the 1907 panic was precipitated by the struggle to get rid of Heinze."[5]

In 1913 the money trust and the 1907 panic were investigated by the Pujo Committee, which recorded the enormous power of the J.P. Morgan firm.[6]

During the years 1900 to 1920 the money trust was effectively controlled by the banking firm of J.P. Morgan, comprising Morgan himself until his death in 1913, then his son, J.P. Morgan, Jr. and the firm's dozen to 15 partners in association with their Rockefeller, Harriman and Kuhn Loeb allies. After an extended documented inquiry, the 1912 Pujo Committee concluded that the "money trust" was;

> *Far more dangerous than all that has happened to us in the past in the way of elimination of competition in industry, is the*

control of credit through the domination of these groups over banks and industries.

It is impossible that there should be competition with all the facilities for raising money or selling large issues of bonds in the hands of these few bankers and their partners and allies, who together dominate the financial policies of most of the existing systems....

The acts of this inner group, as here described, have, nevertheless, been more destructive of competition than anything accomplished by the trusts, for they strike at the very vitals of potential competition in every industry that is under their protection, a condition which if permitted to continue, will render impossible all attempts to restore normal competitive conditions in the industrial world.[7]

In the public debate over creation of a Federal Reserve System in the United States, the 1907 crash was repeatedly used as the reason to install a central bank in the United States. The Fed was put forward as a way to stop financial panics. However, the 1907 panic was deliberately created by the "Standard Oil crowd" and the Morgan firm.

In other words, the same group that *stood to benefit from a central bank created the panic used to persuade the electorate that a central bank was vital.*

How well this private monopoly has maintained its power over the intervening decades since 1913 is the conclusion of a 1976 Congressional staff report. After identifying the closed shop directors of the Federal Reserve System in the mid-1970s this Congressional investigation concludes:

In summary the Federal Reserve directors are apparently representative of a small elite group which dominates much of the economic life of this nation.[8]

What is important to note is that the Federal Reserve is a private system with private stockholders. The money trust of the 19th century has been granted a legal monopoly while almost all other industry is subject to the Sherman Antitrust Act. It is monopoly, and monopoly requires political power to keep in place. It is also noteworthy that writing on the Federal Reserve glosses over the private ownership, yet the very aspect of the Federal Reserve that needs to be publicly discussed is its private nature, who owns what and what advantages accrue to ownership.

Where J. P. Morgan sat on the councils of New York City finance in

1907, David Rockefeller sat in the 1970s and Alan Greenspan sits today. *Wall Street Journal* in 1977 showed how these insiders used privileged Fed information for personal advantage. In 1907 it was J. P. Morgan who summoned the Treasury Secretary for an interview. In 1980 David Rockefeller summons Henry Kissinger for a meeting.

How did the Money Trust pull off this coup -establishment of a central bank under their control in a country that strongly opposed the idea? Justice Brandeis describes the process as follows:

> *The development of our financial oligarchy, ...with which the history of political despotism has familiarized us - usurpation proceeding by gradual encroachment rather than by violent acts; and by "subtle and often long concealed concentration."*
>
> *It was by processes such as these that Caesar Augustus became master of Rome. The makers of our Constitution had in mind like dangers to our political liberty, when they provided so carefully for the separation of governmental powers.*[10]

The J. P. Morgan firm which dominated the Money Trust understood this process of "subtle" and "gradual encroachment" to perfection. The firm even *publicly* opposed the Federal Reserve bill which they had *privately* put together.

The Morgan partners understood this process and were carefully chosen. In exchange for absolute loyalty they received guaranteed opportunities to make personal fortunes from the political and financial power of the monopoly. While Morgan was nominally only senior partner he held final and absolute powers within the firm.

Few Morgan partners entered politics. Most partners preferred to work quietly behind the scenes. In the period 1900 - 1930, four partners were exceptions to this rule and by tracing their political moves we can today identify how they used duplicity to bring about objectives.

These four partners were E. P. Davison, Dwight Whitney Morrow, Edward R. Stettinius and George W. Perkins. In an earlier book we described how the firm of Morgan manipulated the Bolshevik Revolution so the Morgan firm would profit whoever won in Russia.

Morgan partner Davison was head of the Red Cross War Council in 1917-1919 and worked with W. Boyd Thompson, another Morgan ally who aided the Bolshevik side of the Revolution with funds. Dwight

W. Morrow used his influence to get arms and diplomatic support for the Bolsheviks (we reprinted a Morrow memorandum on this in *Bolshevik Revolution)*. Thomas Lamont used his influence in London to soften the British position against the Bolsheviks.

Yet the Morgan firm and other partners gave help to the White Russians fighting the Bolsheviks and was prominent in the Siberian intervention.

Morrow retired from his Morgan partnership in the 1920s and after a year as Chairman of the Aircraft Board became U.S. Ambassador to Mexico (1927-1930) and a United States Senator in 1931. Stettinius supervised *all* war purchases for the United States in World War One - to the considerable advantage of Morgan-dominated firms.

George Perkins was a founder in 1912 and then Chairman of the Executive Committee of the Progressive Party - a Morgan political vehicle to split the Republican Party and ease Woodrow Wilson into the White House. David Rockefeller used the same tactic with John Anderson in the 1980 election.

The device used by the Morgan firm to control American finance and industry was the voting trust. The handful of directors, usually three in a voting trust, was selected by J. P. Morgan personally. These directors, members of the Morgan inner group, and the voting directors in turn selected directors of banks and firms.

Thus the voting trust for Guaranty Trust had two Morgan partners: Thomas W. Lamont and William H. Porter, plus George F. Baker, who was president of Morgan-controlled First National Bank. This group selected other outside Guaranty Trust directors, and Guaranty Trust in turn controlled numerous firms, lesser banks and financial institutions.

This Morgan complex was, in 1912, able to dominate Wall Street banks, and so the "Money Trust." Morgan control was simplicity itself, based on a pyramid of power principle. Morgan partners selected directors of major financial institutions, and in return for the privileges of directorship, the loyalty of these outside directors to the Morgan firm was guaranteed. In turn these financial institutions controlled industrial and railroad trusts and combinations. The system worked well in the late 19th century and the early 20th century. This is how Woodrow Wilson and Colonel House saw this "Money Trust":

> I think Woodrow Wilson's remark that the "money trust" was the most pernicious of all trusts is eminently correct...a few individuals and their satellites control the leading banks and trust companies in America...they also control the leading

corporations...[12]

The Money Trust was legalized in 1913 as the Federal Reserve System, a suitably innocuous name that disguises the fact that it is a private central bank.

The history of the system can be traced through three stages: the original plan created secretly in 1910, the promotion of Woodrow Wilson for President by the Money Power and then finally by what we can only describe as illegal passage of the Federal Reserve bill through the Congress.

Representative Lindbergh from Minnesota, father of the world famous flier, was one of the most consistent and ardent critics of the Morgan group during his ten years in the House of Representatives. He is said to be the only man in Congress who read the entire 20 volumes of the Aldrich Monetary Commission. Such a Niagara of words poured over Congressmen raised the suspicion among reasonable people that those interests responsible for it are purposely making it impossible for Congressmen to digest it. Of the Aldrich Banking and Currency Plan, Lindbergh said:

> *The Aldrich Banking and Currency Plan is a monstrous scheme to place under one control all the finances of the country, public and private. It would create one great central association with fifteen branches to encompass all the states....It would admit of no membership except banks and trust companies, and exclude the smaller ones of these. The rest of the world would not only be excluded from holding stock, but by the nature of the association, powers and relations of finances to commerce, it would dictate the terms on which business should be done. With that power centered in the great city banks and these banks controlled by the trusts and money powers, the politics as well as the business of the country would be under its dictation.*[13]

The Money Trust Creates The Fed

Chart 7 – 1;

STAGE ONE: THE ORIGINAL PLAN FOR A FEDERAL RESERVE SYSTEM

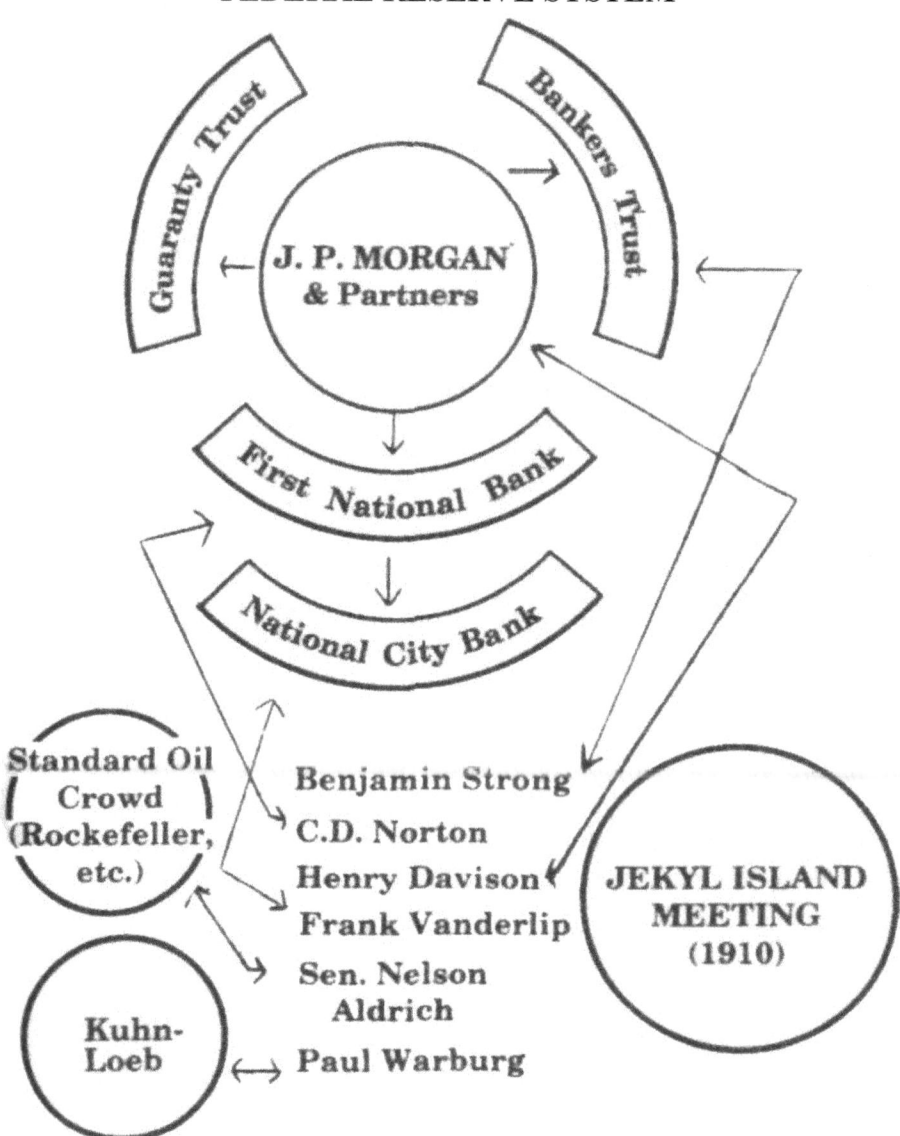

- Guaranty Trust
- Bankers Trust
- J. P. MORGAN & Partners
- First National Bank
- National City Bank
- Standard Oil Crowd (Rockefeller, etc.)
- Kuhn-Loeb
- Benjamin Strong
- C.D. Norton
- Henry Davison
- Frank Vanderlip
- Sen. Nelson Aldrich
- Paul Warburg
- JEKYL ISLAND MEETING (1910)

Endnotes to Chapter Seven

(1) Louis D. Brandeis, *Other People's Money; and How Bankers Use It,* (New York: Frederick A. Stokes Co.) p. 1.

(2) Joseph P. Tumulty, *Woodrow Wilson as I Knew Him* (New York: Doubleday, 1921).

(3) John Moody, *The Trust About The Trusts* (New York: Moody Publishing Company, 1904).

(4) Clarence W. Barron, *They Told Barron* (New York: Harper & Brothers, 1930).

(5) *Dictionary of American Biography,* Frederick Heinze. The Engineering and Mining Journal commented, "This was the beginning of the panic of 1907."

(6) U.S. Congress, House of Representatives, Committee on Banking and Currency. *Money Trust Investigation* (Washington, D.C., 1913) and Committee to Investigate the Concentration of Control of Money and Credit, *Report.* (62nd Congress, 3rd session. House Report No. 1593), known as the Pujo Committee Report.

(7) *The Story Of Our Money,* p. 187.

(8) U.S. Congress, House of Representatives, Committee on Banking, Currency and Housing. *Federal Reserve Directors: A Study of Corporate and Banking Influence.* August, 1976. (94th Congress, 2nd session). Washington, U.S. Government Printing Office, 1976.

(9) See *Wall Street Journal,* August 29, 1977.

(10) *The Story of Our Money, op. cit.,* pp. 188-89.

(11) Antony Sutton, *Wall Street and the Bolshevik Revolution* (New Rochelle, New York: Arlington House, 1974). See particularly pages 89-100 and the chapter, "J. P. Morgan gives a little help to the other side."

(12) Colonel E. M. House to Senator Culbertson (July 26, 1911); Charles Seymour, *The Intimate Papers of Colonel House,* (Boston and New York: Houghton Mifflin Co., 1926-28), I. 159.

(13) Cited in *The Story of Our Money, op. cit.,* p. 189

Chapter Eight

THE JEKYL ISLAND CONSPIRACY

In 1910 six prominent Wall Street financial men met on Jekyll Island to map plans for a central banking system in the United States. The Federal Reserve System originated in a conspiracy. A "conspiracy" is defined legally as a *secret* meeting for an *illegal* purpose. The meeting was secret, it involved six persons and it was illegal...as we shall show later.

The six conspirators were:

Senator Nelson Aldrich, father-in-law of John D. Rockefeller, Jr.

German banker Paul Warburg, of the German bankers MM Warburg of Hamburg and Kuhn Loeb in the United States;

Henry P. Davison, partner in J. P. Morgan and Chairman of Bankers Trust Company;

Benjamin Strong, Vice President of Bankers Trust; Frank Vanderlip, Chairman of National City Bank; Charles D. Norton, President of First National Bank.

The last three banks were in the Morgan group; Warburg represented Kuhn-Loeb and Aldrich represented Rockefeller interests and the "Standard Oil crowd." The Harriman interest in Guaranty Trust had been absorbed into the Morgan group after the death of Harriman.

These six dominated wealth and financial power and had considerable political influence.

The secret Jekyll Island meeting was actually described in *conspiratorial* terms by one of the participants:

> Despite my views about the value to society of greater publicity for the affairs of corporations, there was an occasion, near the close of 1910, when I was as secretive, indeed as furtive, as any conspirator. None of us who participated felt that we were conspirators; on the contrary we felt we were engaged in a patriotic work. We were trying to plan a mechanism that would

correct the weaknesses of our banking system as revealed under the strains and pressures of the panic of 1907. I do not feel it is any exaggeration to speak of our secret expedition to Jekyll Island as the occasion of the actual conception of what eventually became the Federal Reserve System.[1]

After the 1907 panic plans were formulated to convince the public of a "need" for a central bank. The key at this point was Senator Nelson Aldrich, a wealthy businessman linked to the Rockefeller family through marriage of his daughter Abby to John D. Rockefeller Jr. Former Vice President Nelson Rockefeller was a direct descendent of this branch of the Rockefeller family.

In the post-1907 panic era, Senator Aldrich headed a Senate Monetary Commission which toured Europe to discuss and study European central banks and especially the German Reichsbank system. From this junket Aldrich emerged as *the* Congressional expert on bank planning. Few spotted his close links with the banking interests.[2] Herbert L. Satterlee was Morgan's son-in-law and, from the inside, comments on Aldrich's close relations with the Money Trust and planning for the Federal Reserve System. Aldrich, according to Satterlee,

...turned to Mr. Morgan for advice and then during the next two years they were to spend many hours together working out an orderly pattern for the banking world of this country from coast to coast.[3]

Again, according to Satterlee, J. P. Morgan "lent him (Aldrich) Harry Davison (Morgan partner) to help with details while Paul M. Warburg, the Kuhn Loeb partner, also "put his service at Senator Aldrich's disposal."[4] This triad -Morgan-Aldrich-Warburg - was the focal point for planning the introduction of central banking to the United States.

The remaining Jekyll Island conspirators came on the scene later. Frank Vanderlip (whom we have already quoted) of National City Bank was linked to the Rockefeller family by marriage and came into the group in early 1910 after receiving a letter from Stillman, founder and chairman of National City Bank. This letter referred to a meeting between Stillman and Aldrich in Europe on the central bank question. From this letter we learn that the conspirators used a code and that Aldrich's code name was "Zivil." In his book, Vanderlip states:

Mr. Stillman wrote me that I should make everything else subservient to giving my whole time and thought to a thorough

consideration of the subject (i.e., the currency plan) and to draft a bill for the new Congress without a Wall Street tag.(5)

Above all the conspirators knew they had to maintain absolute secrecy. If any Wall Street name ever became attached to a central banking Federal Reserve bill it would be the kiss of death. Not only were code names adopted but individuals went to great lengths to avoid public knowledge of their meetings and discussions.

Without any question if the public in 1913 had known what we know today the Federal Reserve Act would have no possibility at all of becoming law. On the question of public suspicions of the close family links in the group, for which the group claimed disinterested impartiality, Vanderlip noted:

> *But would the electorate have believed that? I question their ability to do so. Just to give you a faint idea: Senator Aldrich was the father-in-law of John D. Rockefeller, Jr., and himself a very rich man. Once I had written to Woodrow Wilson at Princeton, inviting him to speak at a dinner. Wishing to impress him with the importance of the occasion, I had mentioned that Senator Aldrich also had been invited to speak. My friend Dr. Wilson had astonished me by replying that he could not bring himself to speak on the same platform with Senator Aldrich. He did come and make a speech, however, after I had reported that Mr. Aldrich's health would prevent him from appearing. Now then, fancy what sort of head-lines might have appeared over a story that Aldrich was conferring about new money legislation with a Morgan partner (Davison) and the president of the biggest bank (Vanderlip).*(6)

The National City Bank founded by Stillman is significant because one of its directors was Cleveland Dodge, the financial powerhouse and influence behind Woodrow Wilson.

Woodrow Wilson, who was to sign the Federal Reserve Act into law, was a deliberate creation of the Money Power, who was approved in the spring of 1912 at a weekend meeting at Beechwood, the Vanderlip estate at Scarborough on Hudson. According to one observer, Wilson passed the test because Vanderlip and William Rockefeller discussed the role of American capital abroad in front of Wilson.(7) This we shall describe in more detail later.

The central intellectual figure in the creation of the Federal Reserve System was not an American but a German banker - Paul Moritz

Warburg, a banker born in 1868 into the Hamburg Oppenheim family. Warburg's father was a partner in the M. M. Warburg banking house founded in 1798. Warburg's early career was with Samuel Montagu & Co. in London and the *Banque Russe Pour he Commerce Etranger* in Paris. In 1891 Warburg went to work at the family bank in Hamburg and became a partner in 1895. In 1902 he came to the United States as a partner in Kuhn Loeb, and in spite of defective English, began a campaign for a Federal Reserve System. The plan may be found in his pamphlets, "Defects and Needs of our Banking System since 1907" and "A plan for a modified central bank" (1907). In 1910 Warburg proposed a plan for a United Reserve Bank and much of this plan was embodied in the Federal Reserve System.

These were the men who met in secret on Jekyll Island to put together the initial draft of the Federal Reserve Act.

The secret meeting was recorded by Frank Vanderlip:

Since it would be fatal to Senator Aldrich's plan to have it known that he was calling on anybody from Wall Street to help him in preparing his report and bill, precautions were taken that would have delighted the heart of James Stillman. We were told to leave our last names behind us...that we should avoid dining together on the night of our departure to come one at a time and as unobtrusively as possible to the railroad terminal on the New Jersey littoral of the Hudson, where Senator Aldrich's private car would be in readiness, attached to the rear end of a train for the South.

When I came to that car the blinds were down and only slender threads of amber light showed the shape of the windows. Once aboard the private car we began to observe the taboo that had been fixed on last names. We addressed each other as "Ben," "Paul," "Nelson," and "Abe." Davison and I adopted even deeper disguises, abandoning our own first names. On the theory that we were always right, he became Wilbur and I became Orville, after those two aviation pioneers, the Wright brothers.

The servants and the train crew may have known the identities of one or two of us, but they did not know all, and it was the names of all printed together that would have made our mysterious journey significant in Washington, in Wall Street, even in London. Discovery, we knew, simply must not happen, or else all our time and effort would be wasted. If it were to be exposed publicly that our particular group had gotten together and written a banking bill, that bill would have no chance whatever of passage by Congress.[8]

The last sentence says it all from the vantage point of an insider - *this was a planned conspiracy*. The American public would never hand over a monopoly of the money supply to a small group. After all, the Sherman Antitrust Act had just made monopoly in restraint of trade illegal and a money monopoly was even less acceptable.

To avoid public knowledge, these bankers went skulking off to a remote island in the dead of night using code names and disguises!

Vanderlip goes on to describe the secret meeting itself and that Vanderlip and Strong actually wrote the so-called Aldrich report and the bill presented to the Senate. What is interesting is the utter assurance on the part of Vanderlip that the bankers were acting in the interests of the country as a whole rather than in their own selfish interests.

What this group proposed to do - and actually did do in 1913 - was replace gold and silver with a paper factory which they controlled. How this could be presented as a public-spirited act is probably beyond most readers.

> *We were taken by boat from the mainland to Jekyll Island and for a week or ten days were completely secluded, without any contact by telephone or telegraph with the outside. We had disappeared from the world onto a deserted island. There were plenty of colored servants but they had no idea who Ben and Paul and Nelson were; even Vanderlip, or Davison, or Andrew, would have meant less than nothing to them.*
>
> *There we worked in the club-house - We returned to the North as secretly as we had gone South. It was agreed that Senator Aldrich would present the bill we had drafted to the Senate. It became known to the country as the Aldrich Plan. Aldrich and Andrew left us at Washington, and Warburg, Davison, Strong, and I returned to New York.*
>
> *Congress was about to meet; but on a Saturday we got word in New York that Senator Aldrich was ill, too ill to write an appropriate document to accompany his plan. Ben Strong and I went on to Washington and together we prepared that report. If what we had done then had been made known publicly, the effort would have been denounced as a piece of Wall Street chicanery, which it certainly was not. Aldrich never was a man to be a mere servant of the so-called money-interests. He was a conscientious, public-spirited man. He had called on the four of us who had*

Wall Street addresses because he knew that we had for years been studying aspects of the problem with which it was his public duty to deal.

The Aldrich plan written by Vanderlip and Strong did not get through Congress. It was shot down. An ailing Senator Aldrich retired and the Money Trust was forced to look elsewhere to get its plans through Congress.

National City Bank director Cleveland Dodge was a classmate (1879, Princeton) of Woodrow Wilson. McCormick of the Harvester Trust was in the same Princeton Class. By the early 1900s, Wilson, with help from Cleveland Dodge, had become President of Princeton University and Dodge let it be known that Wall Street considered Wilson "presidential material."

A flattered Woodrow Wilson wrote journalist George Harvey in December, 1906 to identify "the influential men who considered him as presidential material." Harvey replied, "naming some of the most influential bankers, utility executives and conservative journalists in the country."[9]

Wilson, for all his public image of a teetering, owlish professor, had one lesson down by heart, that to get along, one has to go along. In March, 1907 George Harvey introduced Wilson to Thomas Fortune Ryan, member of the copper trust and a prominent financier. After this meeting, Wilson wrote a brief for the Wall Street establishment in which he provided academic support for the Trusts -incidentally, in total contradiction to his public statements.

This Wall Street cabal, with the aid of New Jersey political bosses, pushed for Woodrow Wilson to become Governor of New Jersey in November, 1910.

Within a few months, Cleveland Dodge opened a bank account in New York and an office at 42 Broadway to boom

Wilson into the Presidency. The campaign bank account was opened with a check for $1,000 from Cleveland Dodge. Dodge then provided funds to mail out the *True American of Trenton, New Jersey* to 40,000 subscribers throughout the United States, followed by a regular two pages a week of promotional material on Wilson For President.

Two-thirds of Wilson's campaign funds for the presidency came from just seven individuals, all Wall Streeters and linked to the very trusts Wilson was publicly denouncing. Wilson's election slogans promoted

Chapter Nine

THE MONEY TRUST CONS CONGRESS

Congressional passage of the Federal Reserve Act in December, 1913, must count as one of the more disgraceful unconstitutional perversions of political power in American history.

Certainly it is hard to think of any Act that has had greater effect and illegally transferred more monopoly power to a conspiratorial clique. These are harsh words. The reader may judge if they are accurate after reading this chapter: an almost hour by hour detail of the passage of the Act and signature by President Wilson.

The Act transferred control of the monetary supply of the United States from Congress to a private elite. Paper fiat currency replaced gold and silver. Wall Street financiers were able now to tap an unlimited supply of fiat money at no cost.

Yet, as Senator Townsend stated: "This bill did not originate in any party platform. The people have not expressed themselves on it anywhere and at any time."[1] An extraordinary lobbying effort surrounded the bill just as today in the 1990s an extraordinary amount of lobbying is brought forth by any attempt to curtail or even investigate the Fed. In 1913 the Democratic Party leadership came under strong pressure from Woodrow Wilson and New York banking lobbyists to ensure that opposition did not water down the currency bill and allow other private interests to become stockholders.

Witness the complaint of Senator Gilbert Minell Hitchcock, an independent-minded gentleman from Nebraska and publisher of the *Omaha World Herald*. The Bill had come to the Senate from the House:

> Mr. HITCHCOCK: "Sacred document" as it came from the House, of which, as I have said, we were forbidden to dot an "i" or to cross a "t."
>
> Mr. OWEN: By whom?
>
> Mr. HITCHCOCK: And which we were commanded to pass

without a hearing and without much investigation.

Mr. POMERENE: Mr. President, I have been around these hallowed precincts for some time, and I have not heard that anybody has forbidden anybody else to change his views or to criticize any bill that came from the House, or any bill that originated here. Anyone has a right to change his view. The Senator himself has changed his view a number of times. I say that not to his discredit, but simply for the purpose of showing that he has been a free moral agent all these weeks.

Mr. HITCHCOCK: Mr. President...

Mr. OWEN: The Senator from Nebraska did not tell us by whom he had been ordered not to dot an "i" nor cross a "t," and I would be glad if the Senator would disclose that valuable information, unless it is confidential with the Senator.

Mr. HITCHCOCK: I think I will leave that for the country to judge. I will take my chances on it.

Mr. OWEN: If the Senator is content to leave that as an insinuation, it is for the Senator to do so.

Mr. HITCHCOCK: I will take that liberty. [2]

On September 18, 1913 the Glass Bill, the house version of the Morgan central banking bill, passed the House of Representatives by an overwhelming margin of 287 to 85. *Most Congressmen had no idea what the bill was about.* There were no amendments. Members voted for or against, and only the brave voted against. This Glass bill was named after Congressman Carter Glass of Virginia (1858-1946) - a banker (a director of the United Loan and Trust and the Virginia Trust Company).

The Glass Bill then went to the Senate and became the Owen Bill after Senator Robert Latham Owen (1856-1947) of Oklahoma, Chairman of the Senate Finance Committee -and a banker (a major stockholder in the First National Bank of Muskogee).

The Senate took exactly 4 1/2 hours to debate and adopt the Owen Bill, 43 to 25. The Republicans did not even see the conference report. This is normally read to the floor. No member of the Senate could have known of its contents and some Senators even stated on the floor of the Senate that they had no knowledge of the contents of the Owen Bill.

At 6:02 p.m. on the same day the Bill was hurried through the Senate without discussion. President Woodrow Wilson signed the Federal

Reserve Act of 1913 into law.

A detailed review of the Senate debate indicates the Senators had no details to discuss and every criticism went unanswered. Republican Senator Bristow (1861-1944) made bitter comments on the obvious conflict of interest:

> *My allegation is that this bill has been drawn in the interests of the banks; that the Senator from Oklahoma, as the chairman of the committee, is largely interested in banks; that the profits which will accrue to those banks directly will add to his personal fortune; that he has voted to increase the dividends on the stock of the regional banks, which will be paid to the member banks, from 5 per cent to 6 per cent; that he has voted against permitting the public to hold the stock of these regional banks and has insisted that it shall be held by the member banks; and that he has voted against giving the Government the control of the regional banks and in favor of the banks controlling the regional banks, and it is for him to say whether he has violated the rule laid down in Jefferson's Manual.* [3]

The Senate debate, for what it was worth without a conference report, culminated in a test of political strength on Monday, December 15, 1913. At this vote the amendments proposed by Senator Hitchcock - the only Democrat working against the bill - were tabled by a vote of 40 to 35.

Hitchcock's amendments were aimed to make the Federal Reserve System a government rather than a private monopoly, i.e., the control of the Money Trust would be placed in the Department of the Treasury.

It is interesting that the Senate would overwhelmingly refuse to place control of the money supply within the Treasury and prefer to hand it over to the House of Morgan. Colonel House had done his work well.

On rereading the lengthy rambling debate, the likelihood of price inflation was recognized. The argument was a common sense approach that without the discipline of limited gold and silver, the pressure of unlimited fiat money would lead to price inflation. The only argument against was a rather weak "sound bankers would not allow price inflation."

Note that we use the term price inflation. In 1913 the term inflation always referred to "currency inflation," i.e., expansion of the note issue. In the intervening decades the meaning has changed entirely. Today when the term inflation is used it *always* refers to price inflation, i.e., an increase in prices.

The key Senator warning of inflation (currency inflation) ahead was Senator Root, who oddly accused Bryan, the pro-silver populist, as the dominating influence behind the Federal Reserve Act (most unlikely, and a probable red herring).

However, Root did warn of currency inflation and financial panic but then defended the Glass-Owen bill on the grounds that no inflation could come about "unless the sound money men who run the banks brought it about."

Once again we have the Money power controlling the opposition, i.e., proclaiming arguments that can be easily countered while ensuring that the really potent criticisms do not see the light of day.

Today the irrefutable link between currency inflation and price inflation is buried in a confusion of academic double-talk and algebraic manipulation. Today's academic economists are so beholden to mathematical manipulation (with the deluding plea of rigorousness) that they have entirely overlooked fundamental economic truisms. With very few exceptions (Hillsdale College, Ludwig von Mises Institute at Auburn University), academic economic departments are willing pawns of the modern money trust or the Federal Reserve System. (This author can speak first hand of the abysmal ignorance of the UCLA Economics Department in the early 1960s).

The reply to Reed came from Senator Hitchcock, who pointed out that under the Bill, "the control of the currency system of the country would have to be turned over to the bankers." Others like Senator Weeks were unconcerned on the grounds that "the United States has the most competent bank men in the world." But then, Weeks was a banker himself.

The last speech on this Monday afternoon came from Congressman Mann of Illinois, the Republican floor leader who made the rather odd assertion that the U. S. was in the midst of a financial and industrial panic which demanded passage of the Federal Reserve Act.

Tuesday, December 16, 1913

In Tuesday's Senate debate, Senator Root again emphasized the danger of inflation from the proposed Federal Reserve Act. Constant interruptions, according to the *New York Times* (December 17), suggest that supporters of the bill were publicly worried. They argued in reply that inflation was not possible if the securities issued were good government securities - to which Root replied:

> *That is neither here nor there so far as my criticism of the bill is concerned. My objection is that the bill permits a vast inflation of our currency and that inflation can be accomplished just as readily and just as certainly by loans of the Government paper on good security as upon bad security...*

emphasizing the point that;

> *no one denies that in the past from time to time great commercial nations have found themselves moving along a tide of optimism which, with the facilities of easy money has brought them to a point of most injurious and serious collapse.*

Root reinforced his "tide of optimism" argument as follows,

> *...judgment becomes modified by the optimism of the hour and grows less and less effective in checking the expansion of business as the period of expansion goes on.*

He clinched the argument:

> *...instead of doing our duty as the responsible legislative branch of the Government of the United States, we are shirking that duty and throwing it upon a subordinate agency of the government.*

Unfortunately, Root did not push his argument to the limit, i.e., that this "subordinate agency of government" as he called it, was in effect going to be a private money monopoly of national bankers.

The general response to warnings of inflation was to cite the existence of a gold reserve backing for the money supply: proposed at 33 1/3 percent. For example, Senator Williams of Mississippi claimed that the great inflation feared by Senator Root was only a "bare mathematical possibility." Why? Because, argued Senator Williams, "no President conceivably would appoint one member of the board who believed in fiat money." Eighty years later, Senator Williams to the contrary, *every* single member of the Federal Reserve Board and its Regional Banks is an ardent believer in fiat money and an adversary of gold! In President Wilson's era it was impossible to conceive that the role of gold could ever cease. In President Clinton's era it is impossible for policy makers to visualize that gold has any role at all.

Wednesday, December 17, 1913

On Wednesday the powerful behind-the-scenes pressure for the Federal Reserve Act surfaced when the White House announced that it expected the Senate to pass a currency bill before Saturday, that the House would accept this Senate version of the bill without changes and the bill would then go to the President for signature on Christmas eve. The flaw with this hurry-up scenario was that on Wednesday Senator Root's warnings about price inflation had some effect and a Democratic Party caucus was called, during the short dinner recess in the evening, to consider two of Root's proposals: (a) that the note issue should be limited by law and (b) that the gold reserve should be increased to 50 percent with a heavy tax on "depletions" below this level.

After discussion the note limitation amendment was rejected, but the caucus did adopt a proposal to increase the gold reserve to 40 percent while requiring that a portion of regional reserve bank earnings be set aside as a gold reserve. It is interesting to note that the Democratic majority was well aware of the discipline of gold and it was not the intent of Congress in 1913 in any way to reject, or even limit this discipline. In brief, the present day attempt to demonetize gold by phasing it out of the monetary system was not only rejected by the Congress of 1913 but the dangers of any such demonetization were recognized as ominous for the welfare of the United States.

Even after the caucus, criticism was to be heard from a few Senators. Senator Crawford of South Dakota didn't like the private monopoly aspects at all:

> *...you are simply creating a bank of big bankers, a bank to help big banks, but for which you assess the little banks to get the capital. The little banks are simply commanded to carry wood and water for the big banks. You say to the Vanderlips and the Hepburns and the Morgans and the Reynoldses, "come in with your short term paper and get the money" but you say to the Smiths and the Browns and the Joneses from the small country districts, "go somewhere else with your long term farmers paper; we cannot discount it."*

The intriguing aspect of the Wednesday evening is that while a majority of Congress understood more or less the idea that the system would be inflationary, they were apparently unwilling to bring themselves to vote against the bill.

Thursday, December 18, 1913

By Thursday effective opposition had crumbled, and to speed passage the Senate operated under a 15-minute rule. By this device half a dozen Hitchcock amendments were disposed of and others proposed in the previous night's Democratic Party caucus given little attention. The debate records serious doubts and differences of opinion coupled with predictions that the bill would become law before Christmas and signed on Monday or Tuesday of the following week. The opposition was sidetracked. Problems were overlooked. Fundamental questions, including the possibility of inflation, were bypassed by the leadership. One senses almost an air of panic - to pass a "currency bill," at whatever cost. Consequently, although the bill was known to be defective, the *New York Times* for Friday, December 19 ran its reporting under the head, **"Near end of tight on currency bill."** The White House promptly announced that it was considering names for Governor of the Federal Reserve Board. The first name to be floated out of the White House was that of James J. Hill of the Great Northern Railroad. It was proposed by international banker James Speyer - confirming the behind-the-scenes activity of bankers.

Friday, December 19, 1913

On Friday, December 19, the Friday before Christmas when Congressional thoughts were more on Christmas trees than money trees, the Senate passed President Wilson's currency bill without further ado by an overwhelming vote of 54 to 34. Every Democrat in the Senate, plus six Republicans and one Progressive Republican, voted for the Federal Reserve System. Against the Federal Reserve were 34 Republicans. As a sop to criticism, the bill included a so-called "radical amendment," i.e. that Congressmen could not serve on Federal Reserve Boards.

Bankers, not unexpectedly, were reported to be "relieved" by the passage of the bill - but not fully satisfied and still pressed for changes in committee. William A. Gaston, President of the National Shawmut Bank, spent some days in Washington in conference with members of the House and Senate Currency Committees and commented: *"...The prospective conference changes will make the bill more workable for the banks.-"*

Edmund D. Hulbert, Vice President of Merchants Loan and Trust Company, added to this: *"...on the whole it is a sound bill and will do much toward putting banking and currency on a sound footing."*[4]

W. M. Habliston, Chairman of the First National Bank of Richmond, stated, *"It will result in an elastic currency which will avert panics,"* and Oliver J. Sands, President of the American National Bank, commented that

> *The passage of the currency measure will have a beneficial effect upon the country at large and its operation will help business. It seems to me the beginning of an era of general prosperity....*

The only reported objection from bankers came from Charles McKnight, President of National Bank for Western Pennsylvania: *"It will do the country no good...."*

Saturday, December 20, 1913

After passage of the Owen bill in the Senate the measure was sent to a joint House-Senate conference to iron out the major differences between the Glass bill from the House and the Owen bill from the Senate. This conference excluded all Republican members. The conference then met for four hours on Saturday evening, December 20, at which time at least 20 (some say 40) major points of difference in the two versions were uncovered, in addition to minor disagreements in language requiring over 100 corrections. In most of these minor items the Senate yielded to the House. However, *none of the 20 (40) major differences were discussed in this Saturday evening conference, and it was generally agreed that Monday passage of the joint bill was extremely unlikely.* As reported by the *New York Times* (December 21, 1913), "The points seriously at issue embody practically all the substantial Senate amendments."

In an effort to work out some of the major differences, the conferees agreed to meet all day Sunday. Further, on this Saturday the full House met and refused to accept the Senate version of the bill by a vote of 294 to 59 and then proceeded to pass amendments binding on the House conferees.

By Saturday evening, December 20, 1913, the following were some of the principal major points of dispute between the House and the Senate and reflected significant, fundamental differences in the approach to a currency bill:

First - the number of regional reserve banks,

Second - the question of guarantee of deposits,

<u>Third</u> - the amount of gold reserve to be required against the circulating notes,

<u>Fourth</u> - the changes with respect to domestic acceptance in the case of domestic and foreign trade,

<u>Fifth</u> - the changes in the reserve provisions,

<u>Sixth</u> - the right of member banks to use the notes of the Federal reserve banks for reserve purposes,

<u>Seventh</u> - the status of the two percent Government bonds used as security for national bank notes,

<u>Eighth</u> - the Senate's provision with respect to an increase in national bank circulation.

This was the legislative position late Saturday night.

Sunday, December 21, 1913

Quite what happened on this Sunday in Washington, D.C. we shall never know for sure.

What we *do* know is that on Sunday morning the Senate-House conferees were faced with more than 20 (some say 40) fundamental differences on a critically important bill - a bill to affect the lives of every American then and in the future. Yet, the following Monday morning the *New York Times* (December 22) reported on the front page, "Money Bill may be law today." The *Times* reported that in some undisclosed way the House-Senate conferees had adjusted their differences. The "newspaper of record" put it this way:

With almost unprecedented speed, the conference to adjust House and Senate differences on the currency bill practically completed its labors early this morning (Monday 22nd). On Saturday the conferees did little more than dispose of the preliminaries, leaving forty essential differences to be thrashed out Sunday.

The "almost unprecedented" speed in the conference probably occurred at a most unlikely time - between 1:30 a.m. and 4 a.m. Monday, December 22. Let's look at that critical Monday in more detail.

Monday, December 22, 1913

At midnight Sunday, December 21, either 20 or 40 (depending on the source) major points of disagreement required resolution. At 11 p.m. Monday, 23 hours later, the House voted 298 to 60 and passed the Federal Reserve Act. During this brief 23 hours the major differences were reconciled, worded, sent to the printer, set up in type, proofread, printed, distributed, read by every member of the House, discussed, pondered, weighed, deliberated, debated -and voted upon. This miracle of speediness, never equaled before or after in the U.S. Congress, is ominously comparable to the rubber stamp lawmaking of the banana republics.

Mon. Dec. 22, 1913	1:30 a.m. – 4:30 a.m.	House-Senate conferees adjust 20 (40) major differences in the two bills.
12½ hours from conference to printed report	4:30 a.m.	Report handed to printers
	7:00 a.m.	Proofs read
	1:00 p.m.	Printed copies delivered from printers
	2:00 p.m.	Printed report on Senate desks with notification of a meeting at 4 p.m.
	4:00 p.m.	Republican members of conference go to Conference room – to be told that a bill had already been concluded
5 hours from printed final report to House vote	6:00 p.m.	Printed conference report submitted to the House by Congressman Glass – most House members go to the restaurant for dinner while the bill is read (1 ½ hours)
	7:30 p.m.	Debate begins with a 20 minute speech by Glass
	11:00 p.m.	He House votes 298 to 60 in favor of the Federal Reserve Act.

The manner in which the Federal Reserve bill was handled by the Democratic majority and specifically by banker-politician Senator Owen and banker-politician Carter Glass is reflected in a complaint on the Senate floor by Senator Bristow of Kansas, the Republican leader, in which he explains why he would not sign the conference report:

> Mr. LA FOLLETTE: *Would it disturb the Senator to inform us who did participate in this conference and whether any Senator declined to participate?*
>
> Mr. BRISTOW: *As to those who participated in the conference I am not advised. I was a member of the committee of conference appointed by the President of the Senate, but I had no knowledge as to the meeting of the conferees until after the report as it is before us had been made, printed, and placed upon the desks of Senators. I was then notified by the chairman of the committee that there would be a meeting of the committee of conference at 4 o'clock, two hours after this report of the committee of conference of the two Houses of Congress on the bill (H.R. 7837) to provide for the establishment of Federal reserve banks, for furnishing an elastic currency, affording means of rediscounting commercial paper, and to establish a more effective supervision of banking in the United States, and for other purposes, had been placed upon my desk. I, in company with the Senator from Minnesota (Mr. Nelson), visited the room where we were invited to appear. We found the chairman of the committee and the Democratic members of the committee of conference there, and were given to understand that they had perfected the conference report. We were then invited to express our opinion of it, but I preferred to express my opinion where it might appear in the Record, rather than in the privacy of the committee room, and that I shall undertake to do this morning.*
>
> *I see this report is signed by the Democratic members of the committee. Of course, I did not sign it because I was not invited to sign it, and I should not have done so, anyway, for I did not know at the time the report was prepared what it contained, and I had no opportunity of ascertaining what it contained.* [5]

In brief, the Republican leader did not know what was in the Act nor was he given the opportunity to find out what was in the Act. Later in debate Bristow directly accused Owen of inserting provisions for the profit of his own bank.

There were major abuses of the legislative process in the passage of the Federal Reserve Act - sufficient to void the act. If we have a society that lives by rules then there is no Federal Reserve Act.

Both Finance Committee Chairmen, Congressman Glass and Senator

Owen, had conflict of interest with personal banking interests and stood to gain from the bill. Meetings to discuss the bill were held without knowledge of committee members. Decisions were arrived at and established without the knowledge and agreement of members. Major sections of the bill were settled without consultation and railroaded into final form. There is indisputable evidence of outside banking influence upon Congress.

The Federal Reserve Act is, even from our superficial investigation, *suspect legislation.* Most of Congress had no idea of the contents of the final bill and certainly none had the opportunity to reflect and consult with the broad base of the electorate. A private money monopoly was granted to a few national bankers under suspect circumstances.

As Congressman Lindbergh stated on December 23, 1913:

> *This Act established the most gigantic trust on earth. When the President signs this bill, the invisible government by the Monetary Power will be legalized. The people may not know it immediately but the day of reckoning is only a few years removed....*

Chart 9-2
STAGE TWO: WOODROW WILSON IN DEBT TO THE MONEY TRUST

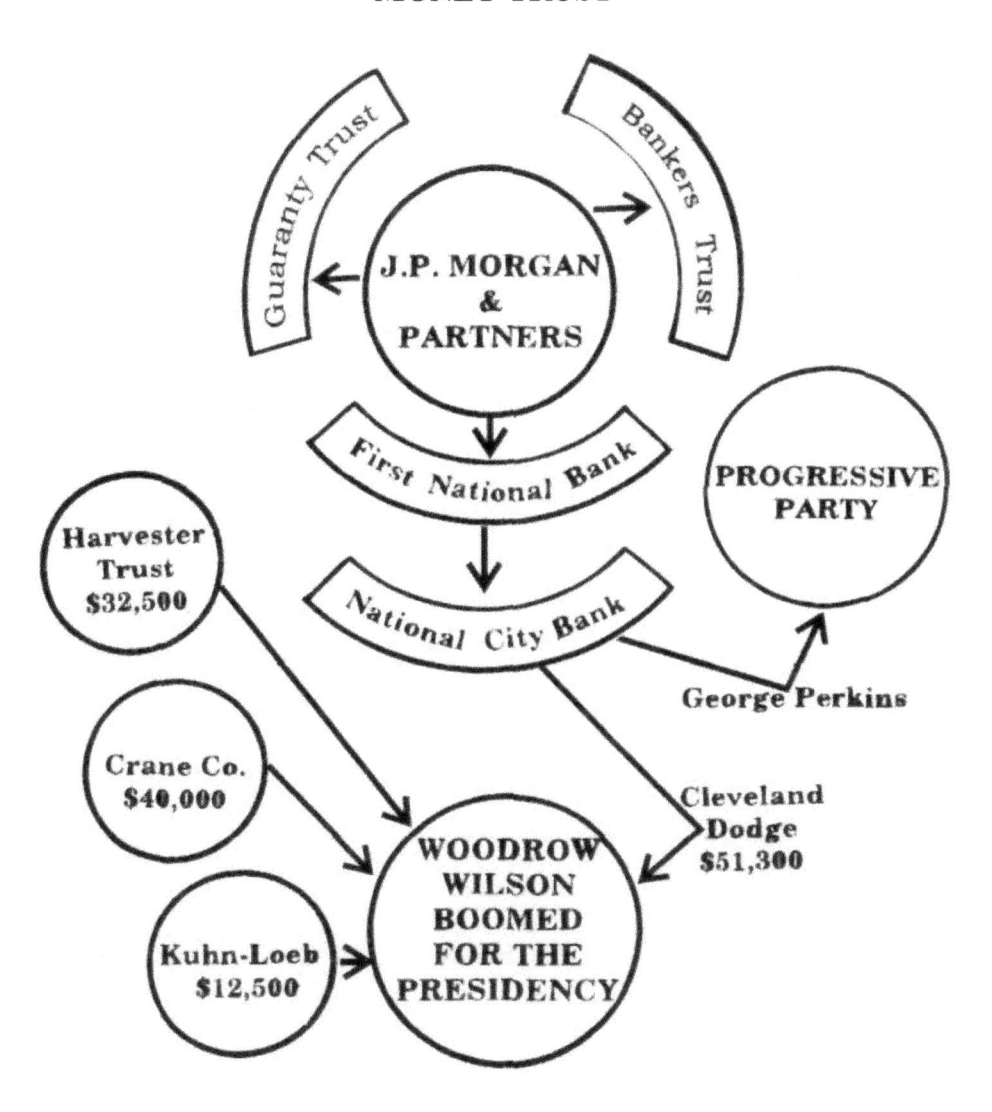

- J.P. MORGAN & PARTNERS
  - Guaranty Trust
  - Bankers Trust
  - First National Bank
    - National City Bank
      - Cleveland Dodge $51,300 → WOODROW WILSON BOOMED FOR THE PRESIDENCY
- Harvester Trust $32,500 → WOODROW WILSON BOOMED FOR THE PRESIDENCY
- Crane Co. $40,000 → WOODROW WILSON BOOMED FOR THE PRESIDENCY
- Kuhn-Loeb $12,500 → WOODROW WILSON BOOMED FOR THE PRESIDENCY
- George Perkins → PROGRESSIVE PARTY

Endnotes to Chapter Nine

(1) *Congressional Record:* Senate, February 8, 1915.

(2) *op. cit.*

(3) *op. cit.*

(4) *New York Times,* December 20, 1913.

(5) *Congressional Record:* Senate, December 23, 1913, p. 1468.

Paul Volcker, employee of Chase Manhattan Bank and Chairman of the Federal Reserve System in the 1970s.

Chapter Ten

THE FEDERAL RESERVE TODAY

Today in the 1990s the Federal Reserve quietly, and protected from any public examination or accounting, continues its never challenged monopoly of the money supply.

Its twofold function is: (a) to regulate the flow of credit and money for specific economic objectives, and (b) to supervise commercial banks, i.e., mostly itself.

The central policymaking body of the FRS is the Board of Governors appointed by the President and confirmed by the Senate. Each of the 12 regional banks has its own directors. These are divided into three classes. Class A directors represent the banking system, Class B directors represent industry and Class C, the public, supposedly.

In fact, Class C directors have *never* represented the public. It is not at all unusual for a banker to serve a term as a Class A director then go on and serve another term as a Class C director.

The Federal Reserve is a private system owned by the banks (see figure below). Fed control over money is a private monopoly granted by Congress.

It's so powerful that no Congressman dare ask simple questions.

Of course, there is good reason why the Fed doesn't want citizens poking around asking questions. It is a moneymaking machine *literally* — and this is freely admitted by the U. S. Government. Here is an official statement:

> *Where does the Federal Reserve get the money with which to create bank reserves'?*
>
> *It doesn't "get" the money, it creates it. When the Federal Reserve writes a check it is creating money. This can result in an increase in bank reserves - a demand deposit or in cash. If the customer prefers cash he can demand Federal Reserve Notes and*

the Federal Reserve will have the Treasury Department print them. The Federal Reserve is a total moneymaking machine. It can issue money or checks. And it never has a problem in making its checks good because it can obtain $5 and $10 bills necessary to cover its checks simply by asking the Treasury Department to print them. (Source: Money Facts, published by the Committee on Banking and Currency, 1964, U.S. Congress.)

Back in 1913 when the Federal Reserve Act was passed, the idea of a Federal Reserve System - in effect a central bank - was promoted to the American people by both bankers and President Woodrow Wilson as an institution *outside the control and influence of bankers* - on the grounds that monetary policy was too important to be left in the hands of private interests. However, in fact, the institution is completely dominated, and always has been, by major New York bankers.

The Fed lied!

The very first meeting of the Federal Reserve Bank of New York on October 5, 1914, was held in the offices of the Bank of Manhattan, 40 Wall Street, New York. Bank of Manhattan later merged with Chase National to become Chase Manhattan Bank.

Skipping intervening history for lack of space, we also find that in the mid-1970s, the leading Class A director of the New York Fed was none other than Chairman of the Trilateral Commission - David Rockefeller. David's term expired in 1976 and he was replaced by the chairman of Morgan Guaranty Trust. However, David's influence was perpetuated in two ways: by appointment of Trilateral Paul Volcker as president of the New York Federal Reserve Bank, a permanent position not subject to the necessity of re-election at periodic intervals and appointment of G. William Miller (member of the Chase Advisory Board) as Chairman of the Federal Reserve System, replacing Trilateralist Arthur Burns.

Moreover, others (of the nine) Federal Reserve Bank of New York directors had links to Chase Manhattan Bank. For example, the three Class B directors were Maurice F. Granville, Chairman of the board of Texaco; William S. Sneath, Chairman of the Board of Union Carbide; and John R. Mulhearn, President of New York Telephone.

Let's look briefly at the career of Paul Volcker, former president of the New York Federal Reserve Bank. In 30 years, Volcker has divided his time almost equally between the Federal Reserve Bank, Chase Manhattan Bank and sub-cabinet positions in Washington, D.C. - a perfect example of the so-called "revolving door" and the Trilateral objective of "blurring the distinctions between public and private institutions" for Trilateral advantage.

Paul Volcker was born in 1927 in New Jersey. His first degree is from Princeton, his M.A. from Harvard and his post-graduate work from the London School of Economics - that well known home of British socialism. In 1952, straight from the London School of Economics, Volcker joined the Federal Reserve Bank of New York as an economist. He stayed for five years, until 1957, at which time Volcker moved from Liberty Street to become an economist for Chase Manhattan Bank, where he stayed for four years, until 1961. In 1961, Volcker went to the Treasury Department in Washington, thus completing the first round of his three stop "revolving door." Appointed as Deputy Undersecretary for Monetary Affairs, he held that job just long enough to learn the ropes in Washington, and returned to New York, to Chase Manhattan Bank, as Vice President in charge of Planning. After three years in that post, Volcker left in 1969 to become Undersecretary for Monetary Affairs at the U.S. Treasury Department. After five years, Volcker completed the second round of his "revolving door" with an appointment as President of the Federal Reserve Bank of New York.

Volcker is also a member of the Council on Foreign Relations, the Rockefeller Foundation and the American Friends of the London School of Economics.

If Paul Volcker was a solitary phenomenon, we could make no case for Trilateral control of the Federal Reserve System. In fact, the Volcker phenomenon is one of a dozen parallel situations.

The Revolving Door Career of
Trilateral Paul Volcker

1952-57 Economist, Federal Reserve Bank of New York

1957-61 Economist, Chase Manhattan Bank

1962-63 U.S. Treasury

1963-65 Deputy Undersecretary for Monetary Affairs, U.S. Treasury

1965-68 Vice President for Planning, Chase Manhattan Bank

1969-74 Undersecretary for Monetary Affairs, U.S. Treasury

1975   President, Federal Reserve Bank of New York

The Federal Reserve Board itself is appointed by the President.

The original Federal Reserve Board represented those very interests that Woodrow Wilson assured the American public would *not* be represented in the Federal Reserve System. The Chairman of the Board was William G. M'Adoo, a prominent Wall Street figure, former Secretary of the Treasury - and Woodrow Wilson's son-in-law. A key appointment was Paul M. Warburg, the German banker brains behind the Federal Reserve System. The Warburg family controlled the Manhattan Bank. Also on the Board was Charles S. Hamlin, of the Carnegie Endowment for International Peace. Another member of the original board was banker W. P. G. Harding. Franklin D. Roosevelt's uncle, Frederic A. Delano, was Vice Governor of the board - very appropriate because the "liberal" Roosevelts came from an old-time New York banking family. John Skelton Williams, President of the Richmond Trust Company was another member. Thus, the initial makeup of the original Board of Governors reflected the elite and the banking interests and from that time on the Federal Reserve System has continued to reflect those interests.

Trilateral Arthur M. Burns was Chairman of the Board from 1970 to 1978, a dominant voice who pretty much dictated Federal Reserve policy. According to Board member and Trilateral Andrew Brimmer, *"Arthur Burns has had a direct hand in selecting every board member."*

Trilateral dominance of the domestic monetary system suggests we examine Trilateral world order objectives for a possible linkage.

Trilateral policy makers and analysts fully realize that the world monetary system, with created money as reserve assets, is in a state of collapse. The *Triangle Papers* dealt with the world monetary systems *(Towards a Renovated World Monetary System)*, and was authored by Richard N. Cooper (later Undersecretary of State for Economic Affairs). Motoo Kaji, Professor of Economics at Tokyo University (author of a book in Japanese, *Gendai No Kokusai Kinyu - Contemporary International Monetary Affairs)* and Claudio Segre, a French banker with *Compagnie Europeenne de Placements.*

Triangle Paper No. 1 identified two world problems: (a), how to achieve full employment without "rapid" inflation, and (b), how to combine "managed" national economies into a "mutually beneficial world economy."

It is vital to hold Trilateralist assumptions in mind. Trilateralists are not looking for a solution to the world monetary problems: Trilateralists are looking for a "solution" consistent with, and which will promote, their own objectives. These objectives are: (a), a managed economy, i.e., managed by Trilaterals; and (b), a "new world order" of these managed economies.

Once again we find manipulation of a problem to achieve Trilateral objectives. Almost on a daily basis we find reflections of the struggle to keep a hold on the U.S. monetary system in order to achieve a world federal reserve system.

Fed Monetizes Foreign Debt

In the early 1980s the Fed, through Paul Volcker, conned Congress into another vast expansion of monetary credit through monetization of *foreign* debt instruments.

The so-called Depository Institutions Deregulation and Monetary Control Act of 1980 is a total misnomer. In practice it brings all banks under Fed control whether they like it or not and gives the Fed power to vastly increase fiat money by monetizing foreign debt, much of it worthless (see attached reproduction from the Bill).

Once again the Fed did everything possible to avoid publicity. Only one Congressman, Dr. Ron Paul, spotted the clause to monetize foreign debt. To avoid any publicity, the

Chairman of the Banking Committee quickly agreed to Paul's request to remove the clause: "You want it removed? We'll take it out."

Then we get a repeat of the unconstitutional conduct surrounding the 1913 FRS Act. The House voted for the Bill *without* the clause - but in Conference Committee it was quietly re-inserted *and became part of the Act as finally approved by both Houses.* We doubt any Congressman knew what was included in the bill as finally passed - that's the influence of the Fed today.

Quietly, without fanfare - and with the vast bulk of citizens unaware - the world bankers have been building an international money machine: an international Federal Reserve System with power to control the world's financial and economic system.

The elements of this global money machine can be traced back to the League of Nations and the Bank of International Settlements in the 1920s. After World War Two the International Money Fund and the World Bank were instituted to globalize credit and loans.

Then in the late 1950s came the Eurodollar market, now a vast international market dealing in deposits and credits denominated in dollars outside the United States. The Eurodollar system may in the light of history come to be seen as a first step in a global dollar system. Eurodollars are dealt in by banks not resident in the U.S. and by institutions not subject to U.S. banking regulations and restrictions.

Paul A. Volcker, former Fed Chairman, has made the role of appointments to the Federal Reserve Board clear, - to support the Chairman's policy.

In reference to Clinton appointment Alan Blinder, Volcker commented:

I think a vice chairman has a responsibility for supporting policy in public statements. If he has any real difference of opinion at the end of the day that shouldn't be disguised but as much as possible he should support the institution.

In brief, the policy created by New York bankers should prevail, whatever the personal opinions of the Vice Chairman of the Board or any lesser Director. *Which is about as close to a closed shop monopoly as one can get.*

In replying to criticism that he spoke out too much, Alan Blinder made a revealing comment: *"When we take actions, they are not reversible by any other body of government..."* New York Times, September 26, 1994.

So here we have it. The Federal Reserve is a private monopoly of money credit created by Congress under highly questionable circumstances which is beholden to the Chairman of the Board and whose decisions cannot be changed by Government or anyone else.

A free society under the rule of law? The United States has quietly become a hostage to a handful of international bankers. And just dare any Congressman challenge Fed authority!

The Federal Reserve Today

Federal Reserve Bank of San Francisco Claims "Some people think we're a branch of the Government. We're not. We're the banks' Bank."

This confirms our discussion in this book.

July 16, 1979 — COMPUTERWORLD — p-139

position announcements

Programmers

The Federal Reserve Bank of San Francisco. Some people still think we're a branch of the Government. We're not. We're the banks' Bank.

At the San Francisco Fed, our Computer Services Group continues to be a model for the National Federal Reserve System. We are using 2 IBM System 370/158's running under MVS/MP. Our software installed includes IMS DB/DC, TSO CICS. Our branch data centers all run DOS/VS on IBM System 370/135's & 370/145's.

How can the San Francisco Fed impact your computer career? Since the Fed is where all the bank regulations begin, our positions will provide you with operating perspective and financial application exposure not available anywhere else.

Applications Analyst Programmer

You'll assume responsibility for design through implementation of small to medium scale automation projects. You should have 2+ years in systems development, working knowledge of OS, JCL, COBOL and IMS and good oral and written communication skills.

Systems Programmer/Database Analyst

You will work with application development teams performing database design and administrative functions. You should have 5+ years in data processing, with 3+ years as a database analyst, experience working with OS/MVS-SNA-IMS DB/DC software equipment. You should be aware of IMS/VS facilities productivity aids, programming languages, knowledge of performance, recoverability and security factors in database design.

If you recognize this opportunity for advancement in your career, we'll be pleased to receive your resume addressed to K. Campbell, Federal Reserve Bank of San Francisco, P.O. Box 7702, San Francisco, CA 94120. An equal opportunity employer m/f/h.

Federal Reserve Bank of San Francisco

Lightning Source UK Ltd.
Milton Keynes UK
UKHW022227280121
377843UK00010B/2500